SUCCESSFUL CONFERENCE
AND DISCUSSION TECHNIQUES

Successful Conference

and Discussion

Techniques

HAROLD P. ZELKO

Professor of Speech
The Pennsylvania State University

McGRAW-HILL BOOK COMPANY, INC.
New York Toronto London

1957

To Gary . . . and to the memory of my dad . . .
both great ones to talk things over.

Preface

THIS BOOK should prove equally helpful to the business executive or supervisor and to the person who leads or participates in any kind of meeting in his social or professional life. It is for the forward-looking man or woman who wants to improve his or her effectiveness in working with others through the conference or discussion process.

The discussion process is analyzed as it occurs in *all* group situations, private or public, and more specifically its application to the *conference* method and to the *public discussion* method. Most books treat one or the other of these objectives. *The discussion process does not change materially as one goes from a private to a public meeting,* or from a conference to a panel discussion. It is the same, but there are important adaptions and flexible applications that have to be made, for example, when a business conference leader changes to the role of chairman of a symposium-forum program at a P.-T.A. meeting.

A well-rounded discussion leader or participant should master the basic principles, methods, and techniques, and he should practice their application in all of his discussion responsibilities. It is therefore logical that these should be put together in one book, both for those who want training in all applications of the discussion process and for those who are interested chiefly in either the conference or in public discussion.

I have tried to set forth a practical treatment of the basic concepts, attitudes, methods, and skills needed to discharge discussion responsibilities. In regard to all the principles, specific suggestions are made for putting them into effect and for readily checking their use.

The approach, plan, and contents of this book have been arrived at after many years of studying, teaching, and consulting in the field of conference and discussion. This work has included considerable examination of industrial and government training materials; observation, consultation, and directing training programs in government agencies and industries; and a wide variety of teaching in university, government, business, and workshop settings.

Although the book is arranged in a logical sequence from private to public situations, and the average reader should profitably study it in this sequence, he could go directly to the part dealing with public discussion if he so desires. He should keep in mind, however, that Parts I and III are also applicable to public discussion.

A separate instructor's workbook has been developed for those who are interested in setting up training programs or instructing. It should be emphasized that in both the book and the workbook, participation is regarded as important a training objective as leadership. We have long since abandoned the narrower objective of training only discussion leaders.

Many people have offered encouragement or specific help to me during the writing of this book, and I am much indebted to them. I should like to extend my deep appreciation to Dean Ben Euwema, College of the Liberal Arts, The Pennsylvania State University, for his interest in my work and for giving me the time to work on this manuscript; to Dr. Robert T. Oliver, Head of the Department of Speech, who has been my friend, colleague, and advisor since my first efforts as a writer and to whom I will always be grateful in all these capacities; to Professors Joseph F. O'Brien and Harold J. O'Brien, friends and colleagues in the Department of Speech, who have read the manuscript and given me invaluable assistance, encouragement, and guidance; to Robert G. Weaver, Training Coordinator, The Pennsylvania State University, for reading the manuscript and making many suggestions for its improvement, and for his assistance in many other ways; and to Dr. Martin Schaul, industrial psychologist and editor for the National Foremen's Institute, for his friendship and his continued advice and counsel. My wife has been patient and helpful during the writing, my daughter Marjorie has helped with the typing, and my daughter Karen with ideas.

In a field as dynamic as discussion, there has been much fine writing in many books which have preceded this one. I am naturally very much indebted to all of them.

HAROLD P. ZELKO

Contents

I THE CONFERENCE AND DISCUSSION PROCESS

II THE NATURE OF CONFERENCE

APPENDIX

I

THE CONFERENCE AND
DISCUSSION PROCESS

1. *The American Scheme of Things*
2. *Specific Group Situations*
3. *Thought Process and Group Analysis*

The discussion process plays a significant part in all our daily living. It is an integral part of democracy and of our individual habits, as much so in business as in our social and political life. The total process is a dynamic one. Both the discussion leader and the participant need to understand the various types of group situations, the nature of individual and group thinking, and the way people interact in groups. We are concerned with these objectives in our initial consideration of conference and discussion.

CHAPTER 1

The American Scheme of Things

JIM WEAVER, average American, awoke this particular morning
somewhat distressed with the state of affairs of the country and
the world at large. He immediately made up his mind that he'd
keep his thoughts to himself and not have much to do with people that day. He didn't realize that an average American just
can't come to such a decision on any average day in our present
scheme of things. And before the day was very far along, he
realized that it was a pretty good way for things to be after all.

At breakfast, his two daughters brought up the problem of
their new school wardrobe, all of which prompted his young
son to chime in with a request for a new cowboy suit. There
followed a discussion of family finances and how they could best
be channeled in order to find solutions satisfactory to all. Like
most such discussions, the exact solution was not found, but
everyone felt that the "meeting" was very worthwhile. Jim was
chairman of this meeting, and perhaps a somewhat autocratic
one. He soon observed some of the problems of the chairman
shortly after he arrived at the office when his secretary told him
that his boss had urgently requested his attendance at a staff
meeting in fifteen minutes.

"Why couldn't the boss give us a little more notice of staff
meetings?" This was the chief thought on Jim's mind as he strode

3

into the conference room. And almost before he was seated, several items of information were passed out and an important problem was presented to the group. After considerable floundering at the meeting, Jim and the others went back to their offices somewhat at a loss to know what the conference decided. No one seemed very well equipped to talk about the problem, and the boss would probably decide himself what the solution should be.

So in the course of about two hours since he had awakened in an uncommunicative mood with the world about him, Jim had found himself both a chairman and a participant in discussion meetings. In his office and around the work scene, he had three members of his staff come in to confer with him about work or personal problems, and he tried to make his usual personal contacts with others during the morning. He also had scheduled an interview with his superior at 11 o'clock, and then he remembered that this was Tuesday, the regular meeting day of his staff. Jim was fairly meticulous about these staff conferences, having sent out a notice to all participants including the agenda of items to be taken up. This was a particularly important meeting, however, since he had to talk with his workers about a new company policy which they could do little about and there were two problems he wanted them to help him solve.

The workday over, Jim thought he'd go home to a peaceful and quiet evening, but his wish was to be denied. Glancing at the calendar, he recalled that Tuesday was Rotary night, and this particular night he had agreed to be a member of a panel with three others to discuss the effect of the new city ordinance on parking. He had some definite ideas about the problems that would be created by the new regulations, but he was glad this was a panel discussion, which did not call for any prepared speeches. Yet he felt a little concerned about the fact that this discussion was held before an audience of about a hundred people.

Arriving home a bit tired and determined to carry out his early morning wish not to talk to people, he had time to take off his coat when the doorbell rang and his wife admitted two members of the P.-T.A. They were part of a committee which was to make a recommendation concerning the school lunch program. This informal committee discussion was rather relaxed and interesting, and after a consensus was reached on a specific proposal, the job was done and Jim could relax in the solitude he had sought all day. He couldn't help reflecting, as he sat down to read the evening paper, that this was a pretty good world to live in after all and that no individual in it could escape to his own isolated island of thought or action for very long. *Rather he should realize how closely related we all are to each other and how much our daily living involves the exchange of ideas with others through the discussion process.*

Discussion in Democracy

Most of us are like Jim Weaver in that we don't begin to realize how large a part discussion plays in our lives. We therefore take it for granted that we can adequately discharge our responsibilities as discussion leaders and participants. Yet a statement by an outstanding educator that "few people know how to carry on a meeting—the Boy Scouts usually have better meetings than most of us," would seem to describe our average abilities more accurately. And a look at the world about us should convince us that our responsibility to use the discussion process to the best of our ability is an increasing challenge to our democratic way of life.

The concept of the world growing smaller is a twentieth-century phenomenon which we take for granted. Although this has come about largely through technological advances in travel facilities and electronics, the world has also drawn closer together through the desire of people to understand each other regardless of where we live on the face of the globe. The nations and the peoples of the world have therefore grown closer together, and the great world forum of the United Nations is the basic symbol of the use of the discussion process to achieve better world understanding. A troubled world with its problems and tensions has made it more essential that we strive for the understanding that can come about only through talking things over. So it is that the average man today seeks ways and means to accomplish this objective.

This is an age of communication. There is no substitute for the discussion process in bringing about our objective of understanding through communication. Starting with the United Nations and other major conferences on a world diplomatic level, we can follow through our desire to understand and live with our neighbors in France, England, Korea, Russia, China, and Japan with an even more zealous desire to keep informed about and participate in the affairs of our own democracy. This is reflected in at least three major areas: government and politics, social and family relations, and business and industry.

In *government and politics,* the average man finds himself trying to keep in much closer touch with issues, problems, and legislation than his predecessor of previous generations. Washington and the affairs of Congress are almost a part of the household, through the medium of television and radio. We like to feel that we know what is going on and that we are capable of taking part in the ultimate outcome. Congressmen and Senators and other public officials report more frequently to their constituents and, more important, are compelled to try to reflect more the thinking and opinion of the people they represent. Through a variety of groups serving as discussion mediums, all of us can be participants in talking over the issues of the day and making our thoughts known to those who represent us. It is becoming common practice for associations, organizations, conventions, and clubs to include in their programs discussions of pertinent problems of the nation, state, and community. Literally, our government takes on more and more of the characteristics of true democracy as the *participation* of all of us increases through the discussion process.

In our *social and family relations,* our use of discussion is constant and limitless. As social psychologists and others suggest a free and more permissive expression of thought, feelings, and opinions among a family group for better family and marital relations, so have we recognized the value of free and open discussion in most of our social relations with others. Even for its value in the home alone, it behooves the average man to become more expert as a discussion leader and participant. And as he leaves the home and enters into a myriad of varied social situations that make increasing demands on his ability to exchange ideas with others, he realizes that none of us can escape the experiences of Jim Weaver, average American. Luncheon and dinner clubs, committees, and even the golf foursome call for the ability to use the techniques and methods of discussion, sometimes in a more formal and planned sense, sometimes in the informality of light conversation.

For all its use and importance in government and politics and in social and family relations, the discussion process reaches its most meaningful value, in terms of a feeling of economic success and achievement on the job, in *business and industry.* We have come face to face with the fact that the work scene is a part of the total social and democratic environment of a democracy, no less important as a medium for the discussion process than the legislative hall or the club meeting. And we have realized this mostly within the past generation, as our total interest in coming closer together and understanding each other as people has spread to every part of our American way of life. Since the work environment strikes so close to the well-being of all of us, we might examine more fully the part that discussion plays in the business world of today.

Discussion in Business and Industry

Communication in business and industry has become one of the paramount concerns of those responsible for the effective management of business organizations. The need to keep people informed, to draw on them for their judgment and suggestions, and to give them a feeling of participation and belonging is now an accepted part of good management planning and policy. This is a natural part of the modern revolution in management, which concerns itself with the *people* on the work scene rather than the machines they run. True, there is a constant emphasis on the physical plant and the industrial machine, as witness the current growth of automation. But the significant thing about industry's concern for people is that it is comparatively new. And this grows at least partly out of the increasing realization and feeling of all people that they are a more closely knit society in the world at large, in the nation, the community, and among social groups. This feeling for greater understanding and proximity, for wanting to be a closer participant in all that goes on around us, was bound to reach into the work scene and be of interest to management and worker alike.

Research studies then came along to substantiate what everyone already knew: that an informed, participating worker was a happier and more effective member of the work team. When his need for recognition was satisfied, he became more productive. The famous study at the Western Electric Hawthorne plant proved this in startling fashion. A more recent study reported by Fred Blum in his *Toward a Democratic Work Process,* a searching analysis of employee participation in management at the Hormel Company, proves the unmistakable trend toward bringing the worker into closer relations with management. Pointing up the need and current practices for communication throughout an organization are recent studies and surveys [1] by the National Association of Manufacturers, the American Management Association, and the National Industrial Conference Board. These and others have found that *one of the chief, if not the basic, mediums for accomplishing the communication objectives of a business organization is the conference.*

[1] See the bibliography of these and other studies in the Appendix.

The Conference Research Project [2] at the University of Michigan concluded that the average member of middle and higher management spends one-fourth to one-third of his working day in conferences. The average supervisor spends about 60 per cent of his workday communicating, most of which is speaking and listening, which can best be accomplished in conferences. Another study [3] revealed that, among major companies, at least 70 per cent rely on the conference as an integral part of their operations. Some put it this strongly:

Well trained conference leaders are as essential to a prosperous America as new materials, new inventions, better labor relations, or any other single factor affecting industry today.

The use of the conference . . . has increased rapidly during the past decade, and it is now unusual to find a company without experience with this kind of meeting.

Conferences accomplish at least these major objectives:

- To keep people informed
- To solve problems and draw on the resources of the group
- To train and instruct
- To afford a participation medium for the individual

Stated another way, these major objectives help accomplish *downward communication* (inform, train, instruct), *upward communication* (solve problems, draw on, get participation, listen), and *horizontal communication* (coordination, cooperation). Although much is said about the time-consuming feature of conferences, a well-planned conference is one of the most economical methods for passing on and explaining information to employees. Bringing them all together at one time is the chief reason why this is so, while there is also the value of achieving both individual and group understanding. Many who criticize the conference

[2] Harold Guetzkow, ed., *Groups, Leadership, and Men,* Carnegie Institute of Technology Press, Pittsburgh, 1951.

[3] Harold P. Zelko, "Speech and Conference Leadership Training in America," *Personnel,* vol. 27, September, 1950.

method as an information medium suggest that the written memorandum is the best medium for passing on information. True, it is frequently an indispensable medium, but it is often insufficient. And it does not satisfy the well-established employee desire to receive information direct from his supervisor by word of mouth, *orally,* rather than through the printed page.

For upward communication and a *feeling of participation and recognition,* the conference affords the best possible medium for employee involvement with the place where he works. Sitting down at a staff meeting or conference with his fellow workers in itself gives a feeling of belonging to a **work team** rather than being an isolated individual. This objective alone might be reason enough for a regular system of conferences within any business organization. But major companies today have found the medium much more valuable than just to give the employee a feeling of belonging, important as this is. They find that members of any organization have a combined experience and judgment which can help materially in solving problems and shaping policy of benefit to the company as a whole. This is why companies are moving toward the "Junior Management Committee," "Middle Management Committee," and "Consultative Management" principles of management to indicate a trend toward drawing on all levels of employees to get the combined judgment of the work force.

In describing what happens when this is not done, a high staff official in a large organization recently in a personal letter painted this picture of conditions resulting from a top management philosophy that would not draw on and allow for employee participation:

Atmosphere is usually something that is hard to describe or pin down. In this place it's easy. Here everyone is tense and uneasy; no one knows where he stands . . . . There is also the feeling, amounting almost to assurance, that the leadership around here simply hasn't grasped the grass roots approach of moving forward from the bottom up, instead of at the top level only, leaving the rank and file far behind. For example, a sweeping organizational change will be drafted and announced as a *fait accompli,* as though everyone will accept and understand it, when, as a matter of fact, most resent the fact that they were never consulted in its planning.

It is true that subordinate levels cannot always be consulted when higher management needs to solve problems and draft policy. But they should not be consistently excluded, and the conference is the best medium to see that they are not, when properly used.

Business and industrial organizations, and government agencies, have so well recognized the uses and values of the conference method that training in conference leading (conference participation training has been too much ignored) has become a major training objective. Of some 150 companies and government agencies in one major survey, more than 65 per cent said that they had in operation conference training programs to equip supervisors to hold conferences. Among the many outstanding programs are those conducted by Esso Standard Oil, Johnson & Johnson, General Electric, du Pont, International Harvester, General Motors, many government agencies, and a host of others. One of the most significant developments was the establishment of the course in Executive Action by the American Management Association, which includes training in conference leading and participating.

Conclusion

We do not have to go beyond our own individual experiences to recognize the major part that the discussion process plays in our lives. In a world brought closer together, a democracy we want to protect and improve, a social environment that emphasizes our interrelationships, and a work scene where we want maximum information and a feeling of belonging and recognition, discussion looms as a basic and necessary tool in all our living. In business and industry, there is a growing recognition of the value of the conference method in accomplishing these objectives, and a consequent effort to improve the use of the method through training. The remaining pages of this book will supply the principles and tools to be applied in order to develop ability as a leader and participant in discussion and conference in the wide variety of situations in which each of us finds himself.

APPLYING THIS CHAPTER

1. Make a list of the discussion situations you have been in during the past week: at work, at home, in your social life.
2. Notice the references to conferences and to discussion situations in your newspaper on any particular day.
3. To what extent do you find that government makes use of the conference and discussion process?
4. To what extent does a family group qualify to make use of the discussion process?
5. Add up the total amount of time you spent in discussion during the workday. What are some of the faults that can be corrected? Make a list of the areas that might be improved through a study of discussion methods.
6. Which of the four conference objectives are more important to you in your own situation in life?

CHAPTER 2

Specific Group Situations

THE DISCUSSION PROCESS is essentially one of *talking things over* among two or more persons, preferably face to face. Since we usually think of discussion as involving several, or a number of people, we think of the participants as making up a group and hence the term "group discussion." Still more recently, as more and more attempt is made to reduce the discussion process to a science, we hear more and more the terms "group dynamics," "group interaction," "group involvement," and the like. Although much light has been shed on the process of discussion by modern researchers, we know it to be at once both a simple and a very complex method of social relations among people. It is simple in that on the surface it appears to involve merely the exchange of ideas and thoughts of the participants working cooperatively toward a desired end. It is complex in that beneath the surface are all the feelings, prejudices, separate backgrounds, and emotional involvements that make us all quite complex as individuals. And as individuals come together, all of these complexities pyramid in much greater proportion than their mere increase in numbers.

At the outset, we should examine the total process of discussion before turning to its operation in specific group situations.

The Total Process: Discussion Dynamics

The term "dynamic" is aptly applied to the total process of discussion. Among several definitions of this word, Webster says it

13

means "active," "opposed to static," "forceful," "powerful." A true exchange of ideas, beliefs, experiences, and feelings among several people is surely active, alive, and vibrant; and the potential results may well be forceful and powerful. Regardless of the level of importance of any discussion group, its conclusions can represent the most powerful force for influence on the national scene, in the community, in club activities, or in the management of a business.

The total discussion process ideally is a cooperative effort on the part of a number of individuals to work together as a group, through the exchange of thought orally, toward some group objective. It is this objective of fusing and submerging the individualism of each *separate* member into a *group* activity and group process that makes for a combination of interwoven relationships which is popularly labeled today as **group dynamics.** Actually, this is not a new science but rather an extension, in particular directions of research and activity, of a continuing effort on the part of all of us to try to understand and improve this extremely important process of people talking things over through group discussion. Anyone setting out to improve his ability to lead or participate in discussion of any sort, informal or formal, private or public, in the drawing room or the business office, should realize the many factors involved in the total discussion process. As he gives more and more concern to these and to the principles and methods which he can employ for better results, he realizes that he must be at once a practical psychologist, a sociologist, and a good speaker. And he realizes that all this adds up chiefly to *understanding people* so that the greatest possible benefits can be derived for the group out of the sum total of the individual efforts of each member.

A number of considerations can be listed as making up the major concern of the individual who would set out to master discussion method and as making up the science of *discussion dynamics:*

- The individual backgrounds of each member of the group
- The status and position of each member

- The emotional involvement of each member toward the subject
- The relationship of the members to each other
- The status and position of the leader in relation to the members
- The leader-group relationship in relation to the subject and outcome
- The relative amount of leader and of group participation
- The relative amount and type of participation of each member
- The effect of certain leadership methods, tools, and characteristics on the discussion
- The effect of physical surroundings on the discussion

The complexity of the discussion process should be obvious, if one is to keep all these factors in mind and improve his ability to analyze and apply them in all group situations. It should also be obvious that to do all this perfectly would assume a degree of exactness and objectivity in the social sciences which none of us would want to claim. The discussion process at best is an inexact science; it is fluid, uncertain—yes, dynamic—and even apt to be explosive. And so we try to seek expertness as discussion leaders and participants, knowing that much can be gained from a sound application of basic principles and methods and of new findings in group behavior and leadership. Yet we realize the limitations of reducing this dynamic activity to hard and fast rules.

The *communicative process* itself is dynamic and complex in any discussion situation. Any single exchange of thought between just two people as speaker and listener involves many complex considerations of status, attitude, prejudices, feelings, language, and speaking and listening ability. In a group, this process changes so rapidly from one person to another as the function of speaker and listener quickly shifts around the group that reactions of all are quickly changing. As the group situation becomes more personalized and intense, this dynamism may reach a point of highly charged emotionalism which both leader and participants should analyze and properly control if necessary.

The science of *sociometry,* generally associated with group dynamics, comes into use in analyzing and charting the interrelationships among group members. The *sociogram* [1] is a charting of the social relationships, and a modification of this can be applied to the flow of discussion in a group to show the exchanges, the flow, and the amount of participation among the various members and the leader.

The role of the *observer* has also been emphasized by those who associate the study of discussion with group dynamics. The idea of having an individual in the group assigned to the observer role so that he can spend his full time recording and evaluating what the group did is a sound way to study the dynamics of the group and the quality of the particular meeting, and this objective has been with us for a long time. It has come into wider use in recent years as we realize the value of this kind of careful analysis of the group process in order for individuals in the group to better see what they did and how they can improve their participation. It is in part a result of the greater emphasis being placed on *participation* techniques in a discussion training objective, as well as on *leadership* techniques.

Feedback is the term that has come into use to indicate the process of the observer, or other group member or leader, "feeding back" to the group his analysis and knowledge of what they did during the discussion. Again, this is a more recently emphasized evaluative and informative technique which is simply labeling a well-established principle in discussion training of analyzing what the group has done and profiting from this in the future.

The use of *role-playing, psychodrama,* and *cases* has received more attention in our efforts to improve on the dynamics of dis-

---

[1] The true sociogram is based on much fuller analysis and understanding of relationships and feelings than is usually known or undertaken in applying this technique to the charting of discussion, as shown in Chap. 8. The use of the observer and feedback are also discussed more fully in relation to measuring and evaluating discussion in that chapter.

cussion by developing in group members the feeling of greater and closer involvement. These are specialized techniques available to the leader and the group for "dramatizing" the problem under discussion and are very useful under certain circumstances. They are discussed more fully in Chap. 6.

Probably the term that all discussion experts use most freely as the goal of a dynamic discussion process is *permissive.* Ideally, the goal of a good discussion meeting is to make every member of the group feel that he has a "free" atmosphere in which he can express his thoughts and feelings at any time. We shall see in our later analysis of leadership qualities and participation problems that the goal should be sought for in problem-solving meetings, but that there are times and certain conference objectives that do not allow for this in the fullest sense. Needless to say, a dynamic discussion should reach the stage where it is dominated less and less by the leader (or by one member), and it should work for a greater feeling of member security and freedom of expression. This is discussed more fully under leadership.

Types of Group Situations

People get together to talk things over in such a wide variety of numbers, places, and settings, and for an even wider variety of objectives, that it is both difficult and hazardous to make a sound classification of meetings that will be satisfactory for all purposes. Yet it is valuable to start out with an attempt to classify the types of meetings so that we can more systematically approach our objective of improving our skill in discussion.

The *objective* of a particular meeting is a major factor in anticipating the planning, leadership, and type of participation called for. This should always be kept in mind, and we shall analyze how meetings differ as to objectives in later pages. In considering the most logical basis for classification, we have concluded that group situations fall into two major types: *private* and *public.* We are therefore attempting a list of meetings in relation to the private or public nature of the particular situation.

A *private meeting* [2] is one in which all persons present are equally active participants (or should be), with the possible exception of the leader, *and without an "audience" of any kind.* Such a meeting may vary in size from two (as in the case of the interview, which we are including in our classification of "meetings") to an average of about five to twenty, as in the case of most conferences. All participants should be in a face-to-face physical relationship, preferably around a table and in a "private" room.

A *public meeting* [3] is one in which certain persons speak or participate in discussion before a larger "audience" who may or may not be participants, *and chiefly for the benefit of the larger audience.* These persons are physically separated from, but in view of, the larger group. They may vary in number from two to five (only one, as in the case of the lecture-forum), and may or may not be in a face-to-face relationship. Usually the audience is large (more than twenty) so as to preclude a face-to-face relationship of the total group, wherein all might be regarded as equal participants, as in the private conference. The larger audience generally does participate during a forum period, at least in part, after the smaller group has finished its discussion, and it is always "participating" as listeners, an active part of all discussion.

The major types of meetings involving the discussion process are these:

TYPES OF MEETINGS

PRIVATE	PUBLIC
Conference	Panel-forum
Committee	Symposium-forum
Interview	Debate-forum
	Lecture-forum

Group discussion
Meetings under parliamentary law

[2] See particularly Chaps. 4 through 8.
[3] See particularly Chaps. 9 through 11.

The conference, committee, and interview are almost always private and are therefore the basic types of private discussion. The panel, symposium, debate, and lecture, usually followed by audience participation in the nature of a forum, are typical public programs involving the discussion process. It is not equally clear where to classify "group discussion" and meetings involving parliamentary law.

Group discussion as a process occurs in almost all discussion situations, and in this sense it is probably not a form or type of meeting in itself. But occasionally, as in learning situations and in typical "Quaker meeting" fashion, a group meets to discuss problems and issues in public situations where the group itself takes over the discussion almost immediately and without a speaker, panel, symposium, or debate preceding this. Such meetings are usually regarded as public, and we are therefore giving fuller attention to this in Part IV, dealing with public discussion. Some who use the term "group discussion" to identify a type of meeting rather than the process confine the definition of the term to the small interacting group of fewer than twenty.[4] It should be remembered, however, that group discussion to many is simply another label for the entire discussion process, and all the principles and methods throughout this book contribute to a knowledge of the total process.

Parliamentary meetings, using parliamentary law as the tool for the orderly conduct of business, also make constant use of the discussion process. It is difficult to classify the average business meeting held under parliamentary rules of order as a public or private meeting, for they vary considerably, and they may be both. Again, all the principles of good discussion come into use in the parliamentary meeting. And since the objective of such meetings is essentially decision-making, we are dealing with this more fully under methods of reaching decisions in Chap. 8.

[4] For this point of view and for an interesting classification, see Joseph F. O'Brien, "A Definition and Classification of the Forms of Discussion," *Quarterly Journal of Speech,* vol. 25, April, 1939.

Conclusion

The discussion process is both complex and dynamic. It is a cooperative process involving the fusing and bringing together of individuals into a group. It involves a number of considerations of individual and group analysis and interaction, making for the total process of discussion dynamics. The social sciences, psychology, and the communicative process are all involved.

In applying the use of the discussion process to particular group situations, we have classified these as private and public. Private discussion involves everyone in the room as an equal participant. Public discussion occurs before others who may or may not be participants. In studying and applying the principles and methods of discussion, we recognize that most of them are applicable to all discussion situations. Yet we are approaching our study first from the standpoint of their application in conferences, the chief method of private discussion, and then in public discussion situations.

APPLYING THIS CHAPTER

1. Classify your discussion situations of the past week under the headings we have suggested of private and public.
2. Does this kind of a classification appear helpful? Might you arrive at another way to classify discussion situations?
3. What would you think of a definition of discussion as a "series of individual speeches people make to each other"?
4. Of the many factors of relationship between and among the members of a group and the leader, is there any one that you feel will most influence a successful discussion?

CHAPTER 3

Thought Process and Group Analysis

INDIVIDUALS ARE made up of a complex combination of thinking and reasoning ability and emotional drives. We try to utilize and apply our ability to think and be analytical, so that we like to claim that our feelings and emotions do not influence our judgments and opinions. Yet we know the strong part that emotions play in influencing our conduct. As we become more and more involved with others in a group, it is more difficult to think clearly and objectively. The influence of emotional factors is multiplied rapidly in the group situation, so that it behooves us both to know these factors and to apply sound reasoning based on clear thinking as much as possible.

It would be difficult to assess whether a good discussion leader or participant should devote more attention to improving his reasoning processes or to the better understanding of the emotional factors that make us "tick" as people. Though the goal is to be a more logical individual, making the study of reasoning an important objective in improving one's ability in discussion, the need for ability to analyze our own and other participants' emotions may be just as demanding in the discussion situation.

The way our *normal thought process* [1] works when we are confronted with a situation or problem that needs to be worked out

[1] John Dewey, *How We Think*, D. C. Heath and Company, Boston, 1933.

is first to have our *attention* directed to the problem. We look into the *problem* and analyze it, then we look for *possible solutions*. Finally we arrive at the best *solution* and take *action*. In doing this we try to think and reason clearly, while our basic emotional drives pull in one direction or another. This chapter will discuss these processes and apply them to individual and group analysis.

Thinking and Reasoning

Thinking clearly and efficiently involves the ability to be *analytical*, *logical*, and *imaginative* (or *creative*). The goal is to apply the thinking process in the group situation while we constantly analyze and control emotions and prejudices that influence us and other group members. We know that it is almost impossible to divorce the reasoning process from the processes within us that allow our emotions to operate, that reason and emotion do not turn on or off neatly or go their separate ways within us, and that most of our reactions in speaking or in actions taken are a result of both. Yet it is well that we look at the thinking and reasoning process, and our feelings and emotions, separately.

ANALYTICAL THINKING

Analytical thinking starts with a mind that is *systematic* and *orderly* while it is discerning and penetrating. To be analytical, one must go beyond the surface manifestations of a subject, or of what he observes. He must look *into* and find the component parts, what makes up the total, how the parts interrelate and influence each other, and what the basic points or issues are in the given case. The analytical person is acute in his listening, always looking for ways to break down and simplify what he hears. And if he is on the speaking end, he approaches the preparation of his own remarks with system and order. He considers the factors influencing selection of subject, such as timeliness, appropriateness, interest, and importance. The group is analyzed, materials are gathered in orderly fashion, and the agenda and outline for the meeting or speech are developed according to a logical system and sequence.

Analytical thinking means straight rather than crooked thinking. When we don't think clearly or accurately, it may be because we have not developed a systematic approach to the subject at hand, including most of the things in the preceding paragraph, because we have allowed prejudices and bias to interfere with our thinking, or because we have not employed sound reasoning. The goal, then, is to be *objective* and *deliberative,* rather than sensitive, biased, or quick-tempered. Objectivity is a matter of looking for facts and truths and of weighing what is heard in a calm and deliberative manner, as free from emotional prejudice and feeling as possible. Just as we like to think that we are completely "reasoning" individuals rather than "emotional," we never like to be accused of letting personal feelings influence our judgment when we are sure that we have been objective. But true objectivity is exceedingly difficult, and most of us can simply do the best we can by adopting it as a goal of our thinking.

LOGICAL THINKING

Logical thinking goes hand in hand with being analytical, and the one includes or follows from the other. When we speak of a person or a point of view as "logical," we usually mean that it follows from careful analysis and from a well-organized mind. Being logical usually stems from thought that is organized clearly.

The basic components of logical thinking are *sound reasoning* and *good evidence* or *support* for our thoughts. The word "proof" also comes into the picture in any attempt to define the total logical reasoning process. A few definitions might be helpful:

• *Reasoning* is the process of drawing conclusions or inferences (or "opinions") from facts or from other conclusions that have already been established or proved to be true.

• *Evidence* is fact or opinion used to support conclusions or points (arguments).

• *Proof* is the end result of using good evidence and reasoning in a given case.

Reasoning

The most frequently occurring forms of reasoning are (1) drawing general conclusions, making inferences, or forming opinions from observation or knowledge of specific facts or instances (*inductive process*); (2) making conclusions about something specific from an already established generalization or conclusion (*deductive process*); (3) inferring that some result or effect will occur from a particular cause, or that a certain result or effect was caused by a particular thing (*causal reasoning*); and (4) drawing a conclusion regarding a point or thing based on a comparison of this with something that has already taken place (*reasoning by analogy*). As we turn to a brief discussion of each of these forms, it might be well to keep in mind that a *fallacy is doing any of these processes illogically, or simply faulty reasoning.*

1. Most of our present beliefs, opinions, and conclusions about people, things, and issues of the day are based on some form of the *inductive process.* We read a number of books by a certain author (specific instances) and conclude that "All books by this author are good books." We eat several meals in a certain restaurant (specific instances) and reason that "This is a good restaurant," or "This restaurant always has good meals." We read about or observe several strikes in industry (specific instances) and adopt an opinion that "All strikes are bad," or "I am opposed to strikes." And as we go into new areas to explore and we observe new instances and facts, we are continually making general conclusions from the specifics. It is not difficult to see how such reasoning may be faulty if these simple rules for inductive reasoning are not followed:

• There must be a sufficient *number* of instances or facts observed before a generalization can be made about them.

• The facts must be sufficiently *representative* of all the facts
that exist in order for the general conclusion to be sound.

The first fallacy is one of the most common in our reasoning.
We frequently are guilty of forming opinions and generalizations
after having come in contact with just one or two examples or
instances. Sweeping conclusions should be made with caution.
In some subject areas where only a few instances exist, perhaps
some generalization can be drawn from just one instance, but this
should be carefully analyzed. The scientist in his laboratory insists on repeating the experiment many times before he feels that
he can draw a valid conclusion. Actually, the basis for the "scien-

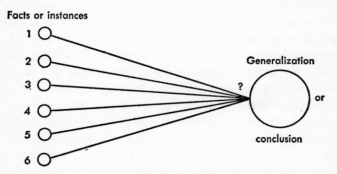

Fig. 3-1   Diagram of the inductive process. Does the generalization
logically follow from the facts known or observed?

tific method" in our thinking is that we develop a practice of
inquiry and *observation* in which we constantly seek as much
information as possible before we draw our conclusions.

An equally dangerous fallacy may be made by observing several
instances that are not representative or typical of the total. An
example of this would be going into a large barn and observing
thousands of "instances" of small, round, green objects known as
apples. From these many instances, one might conclude that "All
apples are small, round, and green." Obviously those he saw
were not representative of the many other varieties of apples,
some of which might be large, red, and perhaps not quite round.

One must relate what he sees and observes to his background and experience, and in this case he would know that the apples he saw were not typical. This shows that the more we develop our total knowledge of things through observation, reading, and experience, the more is our reasoning likely to be sound.

2. The *deductive process* is said to be the reverse of induction, in that we are now reasoning (drawing inferences or conclusions) from the general to the specific, or drawing conclusions about something specific after the generalization into which it fits has already been made. In other words, deduction follows after the inductive process has been used. Going around as we do with our heads filled with generalizations, or having arrived at one which we accept, we come across something specific which we reason fits into the generalization and therefore must have the same characteristics. Deduction, then, is a two-step process after the specific has been observed or contacted: (1) fitting the specific into the generalization, and (2) concluding that it has the same characteristics or implications. Having concluded by induction that "All books by author X are good," we come across a new book by author X and reason that "This is a good book." Advising a friend where to eat a specific meal, we tell him to "Eat at Y restaurant—you'll have a good dinner." Reading about strike Z, a specific and new example of a strike, we say "That's bad," having already formed the generalization that "All strikes are bad."

It is obvious that this reasoning can be faulty, and we must be careful to observe these rules for the deductive process:

• The generalization (or major premise) on which the deduction is made must be sound.

• The specific instance must fit totally and accurately into the generalization.

• The conclusions drawn must be the same, and only the same, as those drawn in the generalization.

There are other fallacies which can be treated in a more intensive analysis of deductive reasoning, as well as there are other

forms of making the deduction. We say, for example, that "Either
A or B is correct." Then we proceed to show that A is not correct;
therefore B must be correct. Again we say that "If we get plenty
of sleep, we will be healthy." Then we proceed to get plenty of
sleep and deduce that we will be healthy. In these forms of
deduction, called the *disjunctive* ("either-or") and the *hypothet-
ical* ("if"), we must be sure that our alternatives are sound in
the former and that our hypothesis is correct in the latter, among
other methods of testing.

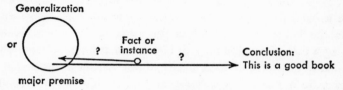

Fig. 3-2 Diagram of deductive process. Does the fact or instance fit
into the generalization so that the conclusion about it is sound?

We usually think of the deductive process as having three steps,
in its formal sense, called a *syllogism.* However, we do not often
use all three steps either in our conscious thinking or in our actual
statement of the point we are making. In the following formal
syllogism of the point about the books, the point may actually
come out something like this, "This new book of author X will be
a good one; he hasn't written a bad one yet." The syllogism
would be:

- MAJOR PREMISE: All books of author X are good.
- MINOR PREMISE: This is a new book by author X.
- CONCLUSION: Therefore, this will be a good book.

Other fallacies of deduction occur when the specific instance
does not quite fit into the generalization. If the book in question,
for example, is by both X and A, it would not necessarily fit into
the circle (usually used to show the generalization in diagram
form), and the conclusion that it was a good book might not be
sound.

   3. *Causal reasoning,* or causation, is a very common form of

reasoning, and the process itself is quite simple. We reason that a particular thing we observe or are championing (cause) will bring about a certain result (effect) or that a particular observable situation now in existence (effect) has been brought about by a certain cause. The former, reasoning from cause to effect, is known as *a priori* (into the future), and the latter, reasoning from a known effect back to the cause, is called *a posteriori* (into the past). One has but to think of the number of times a day he applies this reasoning process to realize that it forms a major part of our thinking. The scientist or laboratory technician knows that a certain ingredient added will cause a certain result. So does the housewife cooking in the kitchen. She likewise, after taking a cake that has failed to rise out of the oven, reasons that the cause of this is that she failed to put baking powder into the batter. So a political speaker reasons that his election (cause) will bring about good times (effect), and that the present bad state of affairs (known effect) was caused by the other political party. It is of course very difficult to establish such causal relations in this situation, where a number of possible causes may be responsible for the state of affairs. This brings us to some of the basic tests of causal reasoning:

• Is the alleged cause sufficient to bring about the claimed result?

• Would not another cause bring it about equally well?

• Will there be no interference with the causal relationship which might cut off the possibility of the claimed result?

• Could the claimed cause for a particular effect have brought this about unaided by other causes?

• Can it be shown that the claimed cause actually operated to bring about the particular effect?

Causal reasoning is frequently based on previously known or determined inductive or deductive conclusions. A physician, for example, from much experience with many cases in the past, knows that a certain medicine will cure a particular illness. He also knows that when a patient comes to him with certain specific symptoms, the patient has measles (deduction). This latter form of reasoning is reasoning from a known effect (symptoms) back to a predetermined generalization (that "All people with these symptoms have measles"), and, once this is determined, the medicine that will cure the measles can be prescribed. This situation thus involves a combination of deductive, inductive, and causal reasoning. Another situation we frequently find ourselves in is, for example, where we observe a condition which is visible, such as snowy-looking substance on the ground in the morning, and we reason that there was frost last night. This is called reasoning from sign, since we observe the sign and try to discern its cause.

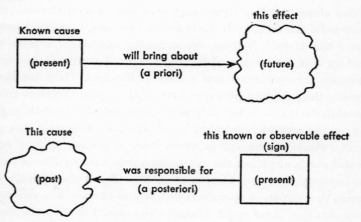

Fig. 3-3   Causal reasoning. Will the cause bring about the claimed effect? (a priori). Was the known result caused by the claimed cause? (a posteriori)

4. *Reasoning by analogy* is the process of making a point valid or clear by comparing it with something that is already in existence or that has worked. The speaker reasons, in trying to show that point A will work, that this can be proved by comparing it with B, which has already been successful. The inference is drawn by drawing the conclusion in relation to the speaker's

point A from the fact that it is similar enough to B to claim that if B is successful, A too will be successful. The analogy, then, is a *comparison,* and it is obvious that the following rules would be applied:

• The things compared must be in approximately the same subject areas.

• The similarities of the one with the other must be uniform and extend to the total parts of each.

• Any one major dissimilarity of any of the parts of the comparison would destroy the validity of the analogy.

• Only the same conclusions can be claimed for the speaker's point that can be shown in the analogous point.

The closer the two items compared are in subject area, the more valid the analogy is likely to be. In trying to make a point about the United Nations, for example, one might reason by analogy that the League of Nations is a similar organization and compare the operations and results of the two. They are both organizations dealing with world peace and might therefore comply with the first rule, but their similarities do not extend throughout, so the second rule might be violated. In reasoning that jet motors would be practical in automobiles by comparing their successful use in airplanes, the comparison does take two items from the same general subject area of motors. But it can quickly be shown that airplanes operate in the air and at speeds so different from cars that these major dissimilarities would destroy the analogy.

It is difficult to prove a point absolutely by analogy (just as it is difficult to insure absolute proof regardless of the method of reasoning used). The analogy is therefore used frequently, more to *shed light* on a point than to prove it, particularly when the comparison is made with something in an entirely different subject area from the speaker's point. This is known as *figurative analogy,* as, for example, when we compare the operation of a jet engine to a blown-up balloon which goes forward as the air is let out; or the three branches of the federal government are compared to a three-legged stool which obviously falls when one leg is weakened. But both in speaking and in listening, we should be aware of this reasoning process and be analytical in our thinking to determine for what reason the analogy is made and how logical it is.

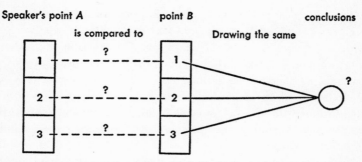

Speaker's point A   **point B**   **conclusions**

Fig. 3-4 Reasoning by analogy. Is *A* sufficiently like *B* so that the same conclusions can be reached about both?

Any attempt to break down and describe each of the forms of reasoning as we have just done gives the erroneous impression that we can neatly segregate these one from the other. Actually, the total process of reasoning is very complex, with perhaps a dominant method used in a given case, but usually with several processes at work at the same time. We can, however, develop clear and sound thinking by increasing our ability to apply and test these principles.

Rationalization is usually considered along with reasoning, although it is defined as "finding a reason" after one has made a conclusion which he now wants to justify. This is quite the opposite of using the reasoning process, the primary purpose of which is to help us reach sound and valid conclusions. To "jump at conclusions" and then try to find reasons for them is a much too commonly used "front" for good reasoning and should not be confused with it.

Evidence and Proof

It is hard to be sure where a discussion of the principles of reasoning should start and that dealing with evidence and proof should begin, for they are closely related, the one leads to the other, and the one depends on the other. If a speaker uses good evidence to make his points, it will usually follow that his reasoning is sound, for much of the reasoning process depends on drawing conclusions from established fact or opinion which is largely what comprises evidence. We frequently describe a person as "logical" when he overwhelms us with facts in terms of specific material to back up his points. And such a speaker usually will be logical, unless, of course, he makes the wrong inferences or conclusions from the evidence at hand. Yet even this may not be poor reasoning but simply his way of interpreting the evidence in relation to ours.

The *issues* in a particular question or subject, which are the basic questions of fact or policy that have to be answered, are usually questions in controversy on which the evidence may bring us to one conclusion or another. On a *question of fact,* such as whether unemployment has risen or fallen in the last ten years, the evidence can determine this absolutely, with no question of judgment involved. On a *question of policy or value,* such as whether the present state of the economy of the country is good or bad (including unemployment), there might be different inferences and interpretations from the same evidence. Good thinking requires that both speaker and listener know when a question of fact is before them, or a question of judgment, policy, or value. There is no point in arguing over a question of fact that can be determined to the satisfaction of both parties by a look at the evidence.

The question of the proper type and amount of evidence needed to make a particular point has some relationship to the degree of acceptance or agreement with the point by the listener. If there tends to be strong disagreement, much more evidence will have to be used before the listener will agree that the speaker has proved his point or used sound reasoning. Proof, then, is usually regarded as the total amount of evidence and reasoning needed in the given point to gain listener acceptance or to insure a reasonable amount of agreement.

The *tools of evidence* are frequently referred to as "forms of support," for their basic use is to support the point being made. Although the use of evidence as proof or support is its dominant use in logical thinking and speaking, we also use these tools to clarify and explain a point and to add interest to the point. *Proof, clarification,* and *interest* are the three objectives of the use of evidence.

Tools of Evidence and Support

> Examples
>> Specific
>> General
> Analogies or comparisons (illustrations)
> Statistics and data
> Expert opinion (testimony)

Examples are probably the most used tools of evidence, for they include any references to events, places, people, and things. A specific instance, a happening, a case are all forms of examples. When we are asked to be specific and to get down to cases, the listener usually means that we should cite examples. In making a point to the listener, perhaps arrived at in your thinking process by an inductive conclusion based on observation and experience, the listener wants you to give him the examples, the experiences, and the facts so that he too can understand your conclusion and agree with it. And the more specific you make your examples, the more effective they will be. When you refer to "Accidents on the Pennsylvania Turnpike" as an example of driving conditions in Pennsylvania, this is not nearly as effective as when you mention and describe specific accidents by date, place, and vivid detail.

Analogies and comparisons have been discussed above under

reasoning by analogy. This tool is usually most useful to clarify and explain a point, as well as to prove it. That is why the word "illustration" is applied, meaning "to shed light." It is well to keep in mind that making a point clear is frequently the most important step toward gaining acceptance of the point. Disagreement often comes from lack of understanding, so it is well to use the illustration freely. Another form of the illustration, chiefly to clarify and to add interest rather than to prove the point logically, is the story or anecdote. A good story with human interest qualities that makes your point, so that you can transpose the point of the story to your own idea, will sometimes do more to gain listener acceptance than a great deal of factual data. And the point of the story need not necessarily be funny.

Statistics and data should be used to supply concrete factual information to back up and explain general statements and conclusions. This includes the use of figures, compilations, tables, and graphs. They should be accurate, up to date, and authoritative, sometimes requiring that their source be indicated to the listener in the event of any doubt as to their accuracy. They should also be attractive, in round numbers in the case of a long figure particularly, and interpreted in terms of listener interest and motivation. Where the facilities provide for this, statistical data will be more meaningful if put on the blackboard or chart (or flannel board or other visual medium) where they can be visualized.

Expert opinion or testimony adds the weight of authority to the speaker's own conclusion in making a point. Usually most effective in discussion of controversial issues where agreement is difficult to get from the listener, testimony is the statement of an expert who is recognized as such by your listener and who substantiates your own point. The value of this kind of evidence depends on the stature of the authority who is quoted, the relevancy of the statement to the point at hand, and the timeliness of the statement. The inductive conclusions we make in our reasoning are frequently drawn from a number of authorities who are all agreed in the direction of the conclusion. The more there is such agreement, the more a speaker is warranted in claiming the correctness of his position. Yet this does not necessarily prove his position, and he should not rely solely on expert opinion to prove a point.

In using evidence of any kind, consideration should be given to the value of *visual aids* in making the material more vivid and interesting. In addition to the blackboard and charts, pictures, diagrams, models, and other visual forms might be used. To make points more attractive as well as more logical in proof will usually lead to greater acceptance of the points. One of the ways to do this is to appeal to as many *senses* as possible. We use the *auditory* sense most in oral communication, and we should also realize that perhaps more learning is acquired through the *visual* sense in most people. In making examples and stories more effective and attractive, we should also keep in mind the senses of *touch, taste, smell,* and *heat* as major doorways to the mind of the listener.

There are certain qualities of **interestingness** that material should have which will also give it more listener attractiveness and better hold listener *attention*. We have already spoken of *concreteness* as being a major factor of listener attention and interest. So also are such qualities as being *striking* or *unusual, familiar* or *close by, humorous,* and *varied*. In addition there is the quality of being *vital* to the listener, which is discussed later in this chapter in relation to motivation and emotion analysis.

IMAGINATIVE OR CREATIVE THINKING

Imaginative or creative thinking places emphasis on going beyond the confines of logical reasoning and thought analysis to explore any possible thoughts or suggestions that might come to mind in connection with a given point or problem. As advanced in his book, *Applied Imagination,* Alex Osborn points out the values of "letting one's self go" in exploring the imagination to bring out all possibilities. Even though this will result in a wide variety of suggestions, most of which could not possibly be applied, the later examination and elimination of each one so as to arrive at the best will bring forth hidden aspects of the problem that should be considered, as well as a better final solution. This means that we should break away from the normal analysis of finding the "basic issues" and of examining a limited number of "possible solutions" in exploring a problem, in an attempt to be more creative and original.

This method of thinking applied to the conference or other discussion meeting where a solution is being sought or policy is being made results in increased activity and exchange of ideas among the participants. The result is a lively and stimulating discussion wherein the most unusual and even impractical solutions may be suggested before critical judgment is applied, with the group realizing that this was being done to broaden thinking horizons. In this way, everyone can break loose from his conventional thought patterns, analysis, and actions which sometimes stand in the way of progress and invention. The proponents of this call such a session "brainstorming" and advocate its use both to develop thinking ability and to open the door for unique or new proposals. The extent to which one should practice imaginative and creative thinking as an individual or in a group might well be a matter of judgment related to all the other qualities of thinking that make up the total thought process.

Emotion and Motivation

As we have already pointed out, it is difficult to separate that part of us which makes up our reasoning process from our basic emotional drives, and the chances are that some of each would be operative in influencing all our decisions and conduct. But we do know that our emotions and feelings play a strong part in all that we do, so that a discussion leader or participant should be aware of them, both within himself, other participants, and the group as a whole. An analysis of the basic emotions should be helpful in making one's own remarks more effective, in determining the possible listener attitude, climate, or feeling in the given case, and in understanding the total group feelings and reactions.

Motivation is the process of trying to move or induce people to feel interested and involved in what is being said. This is a constant objective in all relations with others. One can understand and even agree with the logic of what he hears, yet feel entirely unmoved to be aroused or to do anything at all about it. "Cold logic" might influence the thought process but leave the listener quite apathetic unless he is made to *feel* a personal involvement toward the subject or point at hand. Again, logic and feeling (emotion) are not mutually distinct and separate from each other, so the objective of influencing both can fortunately be accomplished together. The good speaker will *prove* logically that the new proposal is economically sound by his use of evidence in the form of statistics, authority, and example while he *motivates* the listener to realize that it will save him money and be better for his physical well-being. Proof and motivation go hand in hand by linking points that are being made to basic emotional drives, sometimes called the *vital appeals,* or by other labels.

THE BASIC EMOTIONAL DRIVES

> Physical well-being
> Self-approval and self-esteem
> Economic security
> Well-being of loved ones
> Pleasure and aesthetics

Physical well-being is our fundamental drive for life, health, and good feeling. This is what draws us to advertisements that point up the benefits of patent medicines in making us feel better. It compels us to spend money for better-heated homes and warm clothing. It leads us to purchase cars with safety belts and other safety features.

Desire for *self-approval and self-esteem* is a strong urge we all have to be well accepted and praised by others. Recognizing this urge as a real need for workers in order for them to feel like doing their best on the job, industries urge their supervisors to be sure to "give credit where credit is due" when a worker does a good job. In a discussion situation, this can well be kept in mind by any participant who is answering the point of another. If he will give some credit to the other person for what he has said, he will be much more likely to conciliate him with regard to the total point he is answering.

Economic security is a goal we all seek, and anything we see or hear that is likely to help us reach this goal is attractive to us. Many issues that develop in a discussion hinge on the question of economy and how each proposal will affect this. Each member of the group tends to interpret the proposals in terms of his own economic status and security, as well as the "budget" problems of the organization as a whole. A great part of our actions are carried out in the name of "saving money." This drive also includes our desire for professional or occupational advancement which will give us more security. This same desire is also linked to our drive for more self-esteem and "stature" in the eyes of others.

We will go out of our way considerably to insure the *well-being of our loved ones.* This is why we buy life insurance and medical insurance, sacrifice in order to send a son or daughter to college, and join panel discussions at P.-T.A. meetings to arrive at better school systems. Although this drive is most intense within our own families, it extends to our desire to be helpful in the community and to our fellow men generally. The Community Chest drive is successful partly because of this basic desire.

The need for *pleasure* and for *aesthetic surroundings* is in all of us, though probably much stronger in some than in others. We find people occasionally who "work twenty-four hours a day" or who care little for an attractive home, good music, or entertainment. But most of us do seek these objectives, and we look for them in our daily living. And most proposals or arguments which appear purely practical or purely logical can be made attractive as leading to pleasure or aesthetic appreciation. The purchase of a car is linked closely to this drive. There are many practical reasons why we decide to buy a certain car (sometimes they are the result of rationalization rather than logical reasoning), but linked very closely with them is the anticipation of pleasure on a summer vacation, and the enjoyment of the new lines and interior decoration of the new model.

Just as logic and emotion are closely interwoven, these basic emotional drives usually are wound together so that more than one is operative at a given time. In many instances, however, there is one strong feeling in an individual, or in a group, and this can help or retard a discussion. When an emotional feeling becomes very strong, we develop *prejudices* that are hard to resolve, and some of our prejudices do not permit us any consideration of argument to resolve them. Such extremely strong feelings we call *stereotypes,* and they might include our religious beliefs, our love of country, our respect for the United States soldier's uniform. When such a prejudice is wholesome and exists in a group, this can be helpful. But when individuals in a group, or the group as a whole in unusual cases, feel so strongly on an issue such as race prejudice as to make it a major block to successful discussion, prejudice must be recognized and coped with if possible.

Individual and Group Analysis

The goal of much of what we have said in this chapter is to apply the thinking and reasoning and emotional analysis to one's self in order to be a better leader or participant in a discussion, and to the other members of the group. We do the latter both to understand them better as individuals and to get a composite analytical picture of the total group. Our objective here is to try to find out as much as we can, in advance of the meeting, that will help us toward a better discussion.

Group analysis usually starts with individual member analysis, which gradually leads us to some conclusions about the group as a whole. Occasionally the total group status gives us the key to this analysis. This would be the case where the discussion is within or before a particular organization or work group which can be identified. In the work scene, a staff meeting which includes the same individuals all the time can be identified readily as having certain basic background and attitudes. Yet it would be necessary to determine what the attitude might be in regard to the particular subject matter at hand. A Rotary Club group can be identified as having different background and attitudes from a meeting of Local 125 of the United Auto Workers. But a meeting of the Parent-Teachers Association would not necessarily have a "group attitude," since the only thing in common may be that they are all parents of school children, and they might otherwise be quite different as individuals.

Assuming that group analysis starts with individuals, we can set up an objective of finding out what we can about them in order to determine how they think and thus to analyze the group in its entirety. The following are some considerations that might lead to this kind of analysis.

SCHEME FOR GROUP ANALYSIS

Analysis of Individuals	determines	What Kind of People	and	What Kind of Group
Position		Logical?		Homogeneous?
Status		Emotional?		Heterogeneous?
Family		Sensitive?		Cooperative?
Background		Objective?		Interested?
Education		Prejudiced?		Prejudiced?
Affiliations		Talkative?		Logical?
Special interests				Emotional?
				Talkative?

The above table might appear to suggest that the analysis of people can be reduced to a simple series of questions and criteria.

Far from it. We are dealing with something very complex when we try to analyze only one person. This complexity is multiplied many times over when we try to analyze a group. Recognizing this, we can still accomplish a great deal by starting with an attempt to find out as much as we can about the people who make up the group. We start with things that are more readily observable. The position one holds often gives a key to his interests and even his prejudices. So does the level he occupies in relation to others. Does he work with his hands, or is his work interest concerned with supervising others? What sort of background experiences, family status, education, and group memberships does he have that will contribute to an understanding of this person? In the case of the particular membership or objective of this meeting, are there any special interests to help us in this analysis?

We of course cannot usually find out all these things, but frequently just one or two will give us a key to the kind of person and whether he will approach the discussion in an objective and logical frame of mind or an attitude that is prejudiced and with considerable emotional involvement. Assuming that our analysis will not be complete or 100 per cent accurate, whatever we do find out will help as we lead the discussion or participate in it. Then as we put together everything we know about the individuals in the group and our conclusions about them, we can arrive at some group characteristics that should prove helpful.

A *homogeneous* group, made up of people of similar backgrounds and interests, should be more cooperative and be able to arrive at a more mutually satisfactory decision than one that is *heterogeneous,* made up of people of varied backgrounds and interests. It would also be easier to determine in advance of the meeting the degree of interest in the subjects to be discussed when the members have similar backgrounds. This would not necessarily follow in regard to the analysis of prejudices which could exist in the attitudes and feelings of individuals in quite varied degrees even though their backgrounds are the same. Yet,

there would tend to be a "group attitude" in a homogeneous assemblage. There could also be a stronger tendency for feeling of
emotional involvement. Where the analysis leads to the conclusion that there will probably be a variety of attitudes and feelings, the probability might be that a more logical decision would
be reached. This would be because many "solutions" would be
proposed and analyzed, leading to the best "final decision"
reached after a more careful consideration of the pros and cons
than would be likely in a homogeneous group.

Unfortunately, none of these suggested conclusions about a
group will necessarily follow from a preconference analysis, and
any prediction based on such an analysis could turn out to be
unreliable. It must be remembered that there is no "magic formula" to this analysis and that we are dealing with individuals'
feelings, attitudes, and beliefs which are more often than not
unpredictable. But this does not mean that the analysis should
not be made or that it will not be helpful.

Conclusion

Since discussion involves the communication of thought and
feeling among several individuals, one who develops his own
ability to think and reason and to know his basic feelings and
emotional drives should be both a better participant and leader.
He should also be able to apply a logical system of analysis to
any group so that he can anticipate more accurately what is
likely to happen. Good thinking involves the ability to be both
analytical and creative, to use logical reasoning, and to substantiate and clarify one's thought with good evidence and proof. It
also includes a knowledge of the basic emotional drives which
affect our thinking and sometimes stand in the way of it. Group
analysis starts with an understanding of the individual members
of a group to determine to what extent they are likely to apply
their reasoning processes, or to what extent their emotional feel-

ings and prejudices will influence their attitudes and hence their participation.

We cannot expect such an analysis as we have developed in this chapter to be infallible or to result in any accurate conclusions, but it should prove helpful in the given case.

APPLYING THIS CHAPTER

1. What situations have you encountered recently which were resolved by applying the normal thought process?
2. Observe closely your own use of the reasoning processes of induction, deduction, and causal relationship during one day. Note similarly the way your associates use reasoning. How much of this is "sound"?
3. The next time you want to make a complex point clear, try using an analogy to some simple operation which can be compared to the complex point.
4. Read carefully a number of advertisements to determine the type of reasoning and evidence used. To what extent do the same ads appeal to basic emotional drives?
5. Analyze the reasoning used in a newspaper article or editorial.
6. In a social conversation with several people, try suggesting that the group attempt to solve a problem by using their creative thinking to the limit in a free "brainstorming" session of offering possible solutions without critical analysis.

II

THE NATURE OF CONFERENCE

The conference is the basic form of private discussion, and the principles applicable to it are useful in all discussion situations. There are many types and purposes of conferences, calling for a variety of discussion patterns. An understanding of these is essential to the specific steps of conference planning. The successful conference leader or participant learns the importance of knowing his conference objective and of following a systematic plan for carrying it out.

CHAPTER 4

Types and Patterns
of Conferences

IT HAS BEEN SAID that there are as many different kinds of conferences as there are people who hold them. The fact is that the form and purpose for which they are held vary so much that they do not fall neatly into any classification of types. One issue of a daily newspaper recently made these references to news items, all of which include the word "conference" in some form or other:

The vice-president announced yesterday that these two top-level conferences would be concerned with matters of a "normal routine nature."

Nixon, Attorney General Brownell, Presidential Assistant Sherman Adams, and other top administration figures conferred at the White House yesterday for nearly three hours.

Alston [Brooklyn Dodgers manager, during the World Series] met yesterday with his board of strategy to talk over the Yankee weakness and reported he was "very pleased with the conference."

Among the many popular uses and thoughts about the conference method, we find attempts to poke fun and ridicule, such as, "A conference is a group of men who individually can do nothing but who must meet and decide that nothing can be done," or "A conference is something at which, after all is said and done, more is said than done." Yet even such "critics" would not suggest that the method be abandoned. They would imply that it be improved. There may be a tendency to rush too frequently to the conclusion "Let's have a conference" in order to be popular and in stride with current practices. Surely there can be misuse and even overuse of the medium. But, as we have pointed out in a preceding chapter, the need for the conference in modern business practice is very much with us and will probably increase. It should be remembered that the method is a time-consuming one of bringing a total work group into the successful operation of an organization, and our effort should be to find ways and means of improving our conferences.

The Place of Conferences in the Organization

The conference has taken its place as a major medium of communication in today's enlightened management. It is well recognized by supervisors at all levels in an organization that their subordinates can usually contribute a great deal to the sound solution of a problem if given a chance to voice their opinions based on their knowledge and experience. This sum total of knowledge and experience is worth countless dollars to the organization, and the conference method is the best means of utilizing it. Probably the basic use of the conference is therefore in the *vertical* structure, with supervisors at each level holding conferences with immediate subordinates. In addition to *solving problems* through *participation,* such conferences have as their aim passing on *information, training,* and *giving instructions.* They are thus the ideal medium for accomplishing both *downward* and *upward* communication at the same time, for suggestions and decisions made in conference should be passed upward through the organizational hierarchy.

The *horizontal* membership conference also has its definite place in the organization. Such a conference is made up of persons on the same level who are called together for a common purpose and usually led by one of their own level or a staff official. A typical situation might be a conference called by the training or personnel director to discuss with a group of top management officials a proposed new training program or personnel policy soon to be inaugurated in the organization. A group of first-line supervisors brought together under the leadership of a training instructor to learn principles of human relations might be said to be in a horizontal conference.

The more regular and systematic is the conference program in an organization, the better will the method contribute toward the total management of the organization and the development of a work "team." That is why many companies have set up a planned system for holding staff conferences by all levels of management at regularly scheduled times in the week. A member attending a top-level conference can thus pass on to his people whatever he thinks should be taken up with them as the result of the conference he has just attended. There are of course many reasons for *ad hoc* or impromptu meetings that were not regularly scheduled. But they are no substitute for the regular staff meeting, where everyone can plan for and anticipate the attendance and participation he grows to enjoy.

In this respect, those who are responsible for determining policy and establishing a "communication climate" throughout an organization, whether president of the company or foreman, should recognize that conferences take time and allow for such time in planning the workday and the work schedules. The executive who boasted that he "never held conferences that took more than five minutes" actually never held any conferences at all, for it does take time to allow for proper member participation in a good conference. If the rewards of a good conference discussion are to be realized, ample time should be allowed for regular conferences, and they should not be skipped any particular week because of work pressure except in unusual circumstances. One of the surest ways to wreck a conference program and give workers the feeling that management is not sincere in having them held is to give the impression of just going through the motions or regarding them as a frill that can be dispensed with at will.

Another aspect of a planned conference system is the use that can be made of conference reports and minutes, which should become a part of the communication system. The results of a conference, carefully and concisely written, should be passed up

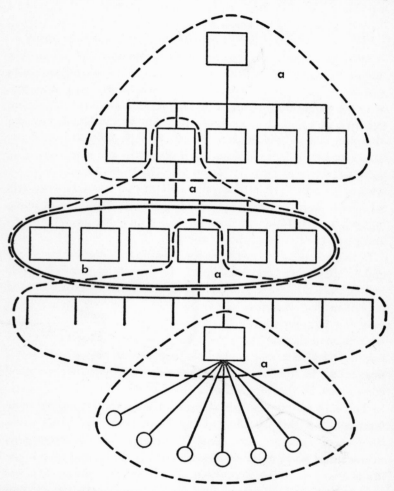

Fig. 4-1 Conference system in an organization. (*a*) Staff or vertical. (*b*) Horizontal.

through channels for whatever use higher levels of management can make of them. They should also be distributed to the members of the conference so that they can have a clear understanding and record of what was accomplished.

Types of Conferences

We are attempting a classification of the *types* of conferences largely from the standpoint of the nature of the group and at the same time setting up a classification of *purposes and objectives* from the standpoint of what the conference aims to accomplish. No attempt is made to conclude that any particular type of conference necessarily will always have the same purpose, although a relationship can be established between some types and some purposes. For example, a training conference purpose is almost always to inform and instruct, a committee objective is usually to solve a problem or investigate facts, and a staff conference may include both information and problem-solving objectives.

TYPES AND PURPOSES OF CONFERENCES

TYPES	PURPOSES OR OBJECTIVES
Staff	Investigate or find facts
Production	Solve problems
Committee	Determine policy
Training	Inform and instruct
Interview	Counsel and advise
Large or multiple	Other or mixed

The *staff* conference is the most common and the most important type of conference in a business organization. This is the conference called by a member of management or staff official who supervises others, bringing together his subordinate personnel into a meeting, preferably planned in advance. In line with the traditional objective of pure conference, that of affording an opportunity for members to contribute and participate and for management to listen, such a conference should allow for participation as a primary objective. Most staff conferences are at least partly problem-solving in nature, where the leader draws on his staff's experience, knowledge, and background to help him in the management of the group, or of the company as a whole if it is a top-level conference. At the same time, the staff conference is an occasion for passing on information or explaining company policy that has already been determined at higher levels and on which a written announcement may already have been made. In the same direction, the supervisor frequently gives instructions to his workers, and these may require lengthy explanation, demonstration, and questions to be answered. Thus a staff conference is not necessarily a single-purpose meeting, and the person who calls and leads it must be aware of the variety of objectives, each of which may require different patterns or methods of leadership and participation.

The *production* conference [1] is one that is called by a supervisor, foreman, or group leader to solve a problem (or pass out information or give instruction) arising in the work scene or area. It may or may not involve the entire staff of workers and usually grows out of a particular situation which requires calling a group together. Although it may be planned somewhat in advance, it is more often of an *ad hoc* or impromptu nature and called without much prior notice. A new production schedule, an unusually knotty and intricate production process, or a machine breakdown may be reasons for such a conference. These would of course be problem-solving objectives, requiring the combined experience and ability of the group. A foreman who observes several workers carrying out his instructions in different ways might realize that there is not uniform understanding of what is to be done. He might quickly call them together to explain the instructions more fully and to insure uniform application by all. The facilities for a

[1] The term was used to emphasize the need for conferences to handle work and production problems by Jack Wolff, *The Production Conference*, Harper & Brothers, New York, 1944.

production conference may have to be improvised at the work scene, yet every effort should be made to utilize the best possible facilities and preferably the regular staff meeting room if it is available.

Committee meetings are usually problem-solving or fact-finding. A committee is usually a more heterogeneous group, since its members would probably not all come from the same work area. Committees are not too common to a business organization as a definite part of the organizational structure except as we find them in companies operating with a "Junior Management" and "Committee" system in which persons at different levels of the organization are brought together for committee deliberations on management problems. It is not uncommon, however, for a small committee to be appointed at a staff meeting in order to look further into a problem. Usually the committee is charged with a very specific responsibility which determines the purpose of its meeting. It is asked to bring in more facts, so that the larger group can better deliberate, or it is told to investigate the problem and recommend a solution for the consideration of the larger group.

Committees also form an important part of all organizations of a nonbusiness nature. Every club, association, and even social group has both standing and special committees. But regardless of the origin of the committee, the meeting resembles most closely the problem-solving conference objective.

The *training* or *instructional* conference is a somewhat specialized type in which the objective is to inform and instruct through the medium of discussion. It is sometimes called a "developmental" conference in that the material to be learned by the group is developed *with* the group. This usually assumes that the members of the group, through their combined knowledge and experience, have had some prior experience with the subject at hand and can contribute to the leader's own knowledge. Training by the conference method, particularly with supervisory and management groups, has become well established in in-service training programs. A group that is allowed to help develop the material it is to learn will be much more receptive to the learning process and much more inclined to regard the material as important and as their own. Since this method is a specialized one, the average supervisor does not find himself conducting such a conference, except on rare occasions. The special skills and tools to be used are well known to the training or personnel director who frequently conducts courses for "conference leader trainers" of selected persons in the organization who will then serve as instructors by this method.

The *interview* is considered here as a *two-person conference,* although it is not a conference in the true sense of being concerned with the discussion process within a group. There are more factors of *interpersonal* relationships than group relationships in an interview, and we do not speak of the person holding the interview as a "leader." Yet it is a type of meeting between two people wherein the discussion between them is the basis of getting together. There are so many purposes for interviews that it would be hazardous to generalize with regard to their objectives. Most interviews follow a problem-solution sequence, this being true of a counseling situation, a merit-rating, a reprimand, and similar occasions for sitting down with another in a work situation. When one goes in to see his superior to sell him on an idea, or when he sells a product to a customer, this is a persuasive interview which tries to sell the "solution" to another person, and again the problem-solution sequence tends to be used. Information-giving is a frequent objective, and also information-seeking, as in the case of a press interview.

The *large* or *multiple agenda* conference is a meeting of a special group, an organization, professional society, or association that extends over a period of time, perhaps more than a day. It is usually opened with a large meeting of the entire assembly which is followed by a series of sectional meetings that frequently take the form of conferences. Actually the term "conference" as applied to such a large assemblage is a misnomer, yet it is used in this sense. Most such meetings are annual conventions or they are special occasions for bringing people together for the discussion of a common subject. A large business organization or government agency with widely scattered locations geographically may bring together at a central point a group of its officials from each location. This could be an actual conference continuing for several days, assuming that all the participants could get together, face to face, in one room. Whether it be this type, or a more heterogeneous convention group, the planner of such a meeting must decide on the subjects to be covered, how they should be arranged in a time sequence, what room facilities are needed, who will chair each smaller conference, and how this can best be put together into a total program. The nature of the discussion within any of the smaller groups varies from speeches followed by questions to panels or symposiums or a pure conference of the group as a whole.

Conference Patterns

The *pattern of discussion* in conferences is the sequence or arrangement of the points that are taken up from beginning to end. Since the conference process is the pooling of the thoughts of a number of individuals, the more nearly the pattern of discussion follows the normal thought process, the more natural it will be for all participants to enter into it. There are two basic patterns, the one following a *problem-solution* sequence, and the other an *informational-developmental* sequence. From these there are wide variations that occur within each pattern, and there is also apt to be a mixture of both in the average conference. As we have pointed out, the true or pure conference is problem-solving in nature and objective, but it frequently has items on the agenda which call for an informational objective. The conference leader, in determining the best pattern for the discussion, must determine which subjects on the agenda are problem-solving and which are informational or instructional. If the conference deals with one major problem and devotes its full time to this, the entire pattern of the conference should follow the problem-solving sequence. Likewise, if the objective is only to pass on information or explain a policy (or a series of principles, as in the training conference), the entire pattern of the conference should follow the informational sequence. And within the same conference where the agenda contains a mixture of subjects to be taken up, the patterns might vary so that in the discussion of each subject a different pattern might be used, first problem-solving, then informational, then problem-solving again.

TYPICAL PROBLEM–SOLVING PATTERN
(normal thought process)

SEQUENCE	WHAT LEADER DOES
Attention directed toward situation or difficulty	Makes opening remarks: States subject (problem). Points up timeliness, importance, origin.
Problem analyzed	Draws from group: Facts showing origin, scope, seriousness, effects, attitudes. Uses questions: What? When? Why? How? Where? Who?
Possible solutions proposed	Gets all possible solutions from group. First encourages free, creative thinking and suggestions. Postpones critical analysis. Stimulates group, using questions, cases, visual aids, possibly role-playing.
Best solution reached	Encourages critical thinking and objective evaluation. Tries for group consensus. Secures agreement. Achieves understanding.

Action to be taken	Determines with group the specific course of action.
	How plan is to operate.
	Application of plan.
	Makes summary and closing remarks or transition to next major item on agenda.

This pattern is called the "normal thought process" because it is the logical way our minds follow through in trying to reach a decision or course of action on any difficulty or situation which confronts us and which develops into a problem. If we adopt a systematic approach to arriving at decisions, we will want to investigate the problem thoroughly, weigh all possible solutions carefully before deciding on the best solution, then adopt a course of action. In the course of doing this, we are also looking for the *stock issues* that are inherent in any situation or problem which requires careful analysis:

Is there a *need* for a change?	(Problem)
Is the *proposal* going to solve the need?	(Possible solution)
Is it the *best solution?*	(Best solution)
Will it bring new evils?	
Will it *work?*	(Action)

Although all the steps in the problem-solving pattern should be considered in the discussion of any problem by a group, it does not follow that each step would always be equally important or would require the same amount of time for discussion. In some subjects, a major amount of time might be spent investigating the problem and assembling all the facts and information that can be brought before the group. Once having done this, a particular solution might be obvious, and all that remains is deciding on the way to put it into action. In another situation, the full extent of the problem might be known to every member of the group, so that little or no time is needed to discuss it, and the major amount of time would be spent drawing out all possible solutions and then weighing the pros and cons. Again, top management in an organization may have decided that a specific policy was to be adopted as the solution to a problem, and the conference of each supervisor with his workers would consider only the way in which his particular work group would put the policy into action. All or any of these considerations would affect the pattern of the discussion, and particularly the extent to which the group went into any phase of it. *There is no exact formula which controls the pattern of discussion, except that this sequence should be kept in mind and adapted to the best interests of the group in the particular case.*

TYPICAL INFORMATIONAL–DEVELOPMENTAL PATTERN

SEQUENCE	WHAT LEADER DOES
Interest and *motivation* toward subject	Makes opening remarks: States subject (information). Points up value and relation to group.
Information (or principles) developed	Statement by leader: Supplies background material. Draws from group: Knowledge, experiences, facts, principles Raises questions.
(Would be done more in a training conference)	Uses cases, handouts, visual aids, role-playing, and other devices from which principles and attitudes can be developed, both by leader and from group.
Acceptance of information or principles	Insures understanding by group.
Application to be made	Points up future use of information or principles. Indicates follow-up procedures. Makes summary and closing remarks or transition to next major item on agenda.

This pattern would be used in the fullest sense in the *training or instructional conference,* and it would be followed only in part in a staff conference where certain subjects were presented for the information of the group. Usually in the staff conference, information or instruction is given to the group directly by the leader, or by a special speaker who is familiar with the subject, followed by discussion, questions, and perhaps consideration of problems dealing with how to put the information to use. The developmental phase in which the leader draws the information or principles to be learned from the group would not usually be used in a staff conference.

Another distinction that can be made between the problem-solving and the informational pattern of discussion is that the former usually calls for less leader control and guidance, for in true problem-solving by the group the leader should let the participants feel free to discuss the subject as they wish. However, he must guide them through a systematic sequence, and this is where his preconference planning of the best sequence should prove helpful. Where the leader is developing information or instructional principles with the group, he tends to keep more control over the discussion, as we shall see more fully in our discussion of leadership in Chap. 6.

Conclusion

Although conferences differ widely in type and pattern of discussion, there are certain basic types and purposes, and it is helpful to the best planning of a conference to determine these in advance. The place of the conference in an organization is primarily as a communication medium to insure communication downward and upward and to draw on members of a work group to contribute their knowledge and experience to the solution of problems, the determination of policy, and the development of information. In this sense, the conference is most valuable as a participation medium toward the achievement of teamwork and a spirit of belonging.

The basic types of conferences in an organization are staff, production, committee, training, interview, and the large or multiple conference. Conference objectives are usually to solve problems, investigate, determine policy, and inform or instruct. In doing any of these, both leader and participants should be aware of the two basic patterns of conference discussion, the problem-solving or normal thought pattern and the informational-developmental pattern. Within these, a wide variation of patterns may be used.

APPLYING THIS CHAPTER

1. What was the last knotty problem in your work or home which you attempted to solve yourself? To what extent might your solution be changed or improved if you called in your work associates or your family to a conference on the problem?
2. In your own work situation, work out a plan for holding meetings at regular intervals. What do you feel would be the best schedule and frequency of such conferences?
3. In an informal group or conversation with several others, see if you can take over the role of leader and direct the discussion of a subject through the problem-solution pattern.
4. What are the values of committee discussions in your organization? Make a list of subjects that might be handled by committees.

CHAPTER 5

Conference Planning

IF WE STOP to consider the many things that can happen to contribute to the failure of a conference, we realize the value of careful planning and preparation. More often than not, the reason for a breakdown during a conference may stem from something that happened—or did not happen—before the meeting started. Even such pitfalls as lack of participation by members, failure to get anywhere, or a bitter argument between two people can be avoided if the conference leader properly analyzes the group and the individuals in it, if he sends them a copy of the agenda in advance of the meeting, and if he makes a plan for conducting the discussion. Then there are such things as uncomfortable chairs, sitting in drafts, poor lighting or table arrangement, or no chalk at the blackboard, all of which are obvious physical faults which need not happen. There is little excuse for failing to plan and prepare for a conference by following a series of systematic steps.

Steps in Conference Planning

1. Determine the *purpose* of the meeting.
2. Consider the *participants, special guests,* or *speakers.*
3. *Analyze the entire group.*
4. Prepare a conference *agenda.*
5. Send *notice* to all who will attend.
6. Arrange *facilities.*
7. Assemble necessary *materials.*

8. Prepare an *outline for leading* the discussion.
9. Prepare for *participation* (if a participant).
10. Plan for making a *report* of the results.

1. *Determine the purpose of the meeting.* This is simply a matter of knowing what you want the conference to accomplish between the time it is opened and the time for closing. Yet it is an extremely important step because much of what follows, both in preparing and in actually leading the conference, will depend on the purpose to be accomplished. Some of the things to consider in arriving at the exact purpose are:

• What subjects are to be taken up? Are there some particularly pressing matters that must be handled at this meeting? Which one is most important? Am I calling this meeting to take up only one major subject, or are there a variety of items? Can this particular subject be discussed fully at this meeting, or should we plan just to open it up and continue it at a later meeting? Shall I want the members of the group to contribute subjects which they feel should be taken up?

• Are the subjects problem-solving or informational in nature? In other words, is this a problem that I want the group to help me solve? If so, should we actually arrive at a decision in the group, or should I just consider their suggestions and make a decision later? Or is the subject one that requires me fully to inform the group by making a talk that will explain the subject and then answer their questions?

• How much time is there? How broad a purpose, or how many purposes can be accomplished in the time available?

• Can this particular group actually accomplish this purpose I have in mind, or is it unrealistic?

These and other questions are pertinent in arriving at the purpose of the meeting. You must know the purpose in your own mind in order to plan further, and you must inform the participants of the purpose before the meeting if you are to expect good participation from them. A common fault of conference planning is to include too many subjects in the agenda, or one that is too complex. Then we have all attended meetings where the leader would not be sure of what subjects were to be taken up and relied fully on the group to suggest subjects. In a staff meeting, it is of course good practice to give each member an opportunity to bring up subjects (it is better to get these in advance, as we point out later in regard to preparing the agenda), but the conference leader who habitually starts the meeting with, "Well, here we are ... I don't have anything in particular to bring up ... do any of you?" will soon lose the confidence of his group for future meetings. The time factor, too, imposes a limitation on the total purpose in terms of how many subjects can be covered and the extent of the discussion on them.

Perhaps the most important aspect of knowing what your purpose is in running a conference is the determination of whether the discussion is problem-solving or informational in regard to various subjects and the conference as a whole. As we have already seen and will observe further, the pattern of the discussion and the nature of the leader's job are quite different as these objectives vary. And even after we determine that we want the group to help solve the problem, we must be sure in advance just how much we can leave the final decision to the group. With some problems, the solution, the action to be taken, and the final decision will be reached in the conference room. With others, the leader may seek the advice and judgment of the group, then have to make the final decision himself or in consultation with his superiors. These matters can be determined in advance, and it all adds up to insuring that *both leader and group* should know the exact purpose of the meeting, what they are trying to accomplish, and the extent of the group's control over the final outcome.

2. *Consider the participants, special guests, or speakers.* Much of the time, particularly in staff meetings, the participants will be members of the same work group and readily identified in advance. In many other situations, the conference leader will have to decide just what membership the group should have to ac-

complish the purpose of the meeting. And in doing this, he must be careful to include everyone who should be invited as well as to avoid inviting anyone who should not be there. It is not uncommon to discover during a discussion that a particular person would be vitally concerned with the way a problem was solved and could also contribute to its solution, yet had not been invited. The same mistake can be very damaging in another way when someone is invited who impedes the discussion and has no interest in it. But occasionally it is wise to invite such an individual if he can profit by hearing the discussion more than he would by just reading a written report of the conference. Such a person might be a member of higher management or a staff official. The chief caution in inviting him, however, is that his presence might be a deterrent to the free expression of thought and opinion by the members who should be actively participating. It may be desirable to explain his presence to the group and to allay their concern along this line.

Thought should be given to inviting someone to join the group as a speaker on some phase of the subject under discussion in which he is an expert or has peculiar command of the facts. This is valuable in the problem analysis phase of a problem-solving meeting, in order to supply the group with all the facts it should have to understand the problem intelligently. Or in an informational or training conference, such a speaker might assume a substantial role. An important factor would be to insure that the formal remarks of this speaker are brief and that they do not occupy a major amount of the total time unless, as in the information meeting, his remarks are the chief material on which the discussion is to be based.

3. *Analyze the entire group.* The easiest part of group analysis is to determine the *size* in terms of numbers of people who will be present. The conference leader may not have complete control over this, but he should do what he can to insure that the group will not be too large. The ideal number for a good conference is from about ten to fifteen, with twenty as a maximum. This is assuming the average length of a business meeting as one hour—

or two at the most—average conference facilities, and a true conference situation in which member participation is desired to the maximum. The degree to which the group will participate and control the outcome by their participation has some relationship to the size of the group. If the objective is informational, in which the leader or guest speakers will present most of the information, the group can be larger, with discussion probably confined to a question-and-answer period. But problem-solving objectives require a group small enough so that there is a close feeling of involvement among the members and so that each member can have an opportunity to express himself fully.

Much more difficult is the analysis of the group in terms of finding out as much as possible about them in relation to the subject and purpose of the particular meeting. Here is where we should apply the principles of individual and group analysis as we discussed them in Chap. 3 and determine what we can of the answers to questions like these:

- What experience have the members of the group had with this subject or problem?
- How much do they know about the subject?
- Will they be likely to contribute what they know?
- What individual members will contribute the most?
- Are there some members who normally do not speak up? Are they likely to speak more or less on this particular subject?
- What attitudes and prejudices may have been formed toward the problem? Are there some members who will definitely favor a particular plan or solution that can be determined in advance? Are there others feeling equally strong in another direction? Will this bring about strong friction during the discussion? How can it best be resolved?
- If the purpose of the meeting is to announce and explain a new company policy already formulated, will the group as a whole favor or oppose this policy? Will they be indifferent toward it? How much does the new policy actually differ from the one we have now? Can we minimize the changes so as to

break down the normal tendency of the group to resist change?

• During the actual discussion, after we have assembled all the facts and analyzed the problem, which members will be most valuable in starting to contribute possible solutions? Can we insure that all possible solutions will be placed before the group prior to a consideration of their pros and cons, or will the group tend to be "argumentative" at an early stage?

These and other questions indicate the complexity of the group analysis process and also its value. If answers to just a part of these questions can be obtained in advance of the meeting, the job of leadership and the success of the meeting have a much greater chance of being realized.

4. *Prepare a conference agenda.* The agenda is the plan for the conference in terms of the subjects to be taken up and the time schedule in relation to each. It should be made up in advance of the meeting and preferably sent to all participants. In a series of regular staff meetings, the agenda for the following meetings is often discussed and even decided on at a previous meeting. This is a good practice in that it is a convenient way to get suggestions for the agenda from the participants. However, it is not always feasible.

The person calling the meeting is responsible for making up the agenda, and he is usually in the best position to determine what the purpose of the meeting is and what subjects should be discussed. In the case of an occasional meeting called at the discretion of the chairman, the agenda is made up by him without calling on members for suggestions. It is well to ask the invited members, however, whether they might suggest changes or additions. This can be done by getting in touch with them (or some of them) informally while in the process of making up the agenda and sitting down to discuss it with them. Members feel a greater sense of belonging to the meeting if they have had a part of this planning process. It will also allay any feeling that the meeting is structured and controlled too much by the leader.

The main purpose of the agenda is to give an organized plan to the conference and to keep it "on the track" from the standpoint of covering the items in the time available. In addition, it gives the members notice of why they are called together so that they can anticipate and prepare for the subjects to be taken up. It behooves both leader and participants to cooperate toward sticking to the agenda, including *starting on time* and *ending on time*.

The problem of *hidden agendas* frequently comes up when either leader or participants feel strongly that other matters should come up in addition to, or in different form from, the items on the agenda. Certain members may want to modify the agenda in terms of injecting proposals for the solution phase of a discussion before the problem has been adequately discussed. This may be motivated by a driving urge to "get this on the floor before Joe does." The competitive feeling between members thus accentuates the problem of hidden agendas. More difficult is the situation where a member insists on taking up a subject that is not related to the discussion because of some personal attachment to the subject he prefers.

The leader may have subjects in mind that he prefers not to list on the agenda so that he may introduce them when he thinks it is "strategic." Or he may strongly prefer a particular solution and try to maneuver the discussion in its direction. These problems deal with leadership and participation and are considered further in later chapters.

More often than not, a business conference has a *multiple agenda*, comprising several subjects of an informational or problem-solving nature, or a combination of both. When it can be indicated, members should be advised whether they will be given an opportunity to help solve a problem and shape policy or whether a particular subject will be presented by the leader or a speaker chiefly for their information. When there are several subjects to be considered, it is helpful to show the time to be devoted to each, but if this is not practical, it can be omitted.

Here are some sample agendas. An agenda for a conference comprising a series of meetings is shown in the Appendix.

CONFERENCE AGENDA (A)

Type of Meeting: Regular staff meeting

Purpose: To explain new company policy and to take up problems for group consideration.

Time: Jan. 17, 2:00–4:00 P.M.

1. Explanation of new company policy on reporting to work
   —Hours and responsibilities
   —Problems arising from this
2. Problem of getting cooperation from other departments
3. Problem of supervisors giving personal advice to workers
4. Special problems of group members

CONFERENCE AGENDA (B)

Meeting of Training Coordinating Committee

Dec. 18, 10:00–11:00 A.M

10:00 Announcement and explanation of current training in progress

10:15 The problem of conference rooms for the supervisory training program

10:30 Future training plans and programs
   —Orientation training
   —Executive training
   —Clerical training
   —Effective speaking and communications

11:00 Adjournment

CONFERENCE AGENDA (C)

Special meeting of workers in Packaging Division

Purpose: To discuss an urgent work problem

Time: April 13, 3:00 P.M.

1. Analysis of problem of package breakage
2. Examination of present method of packaging
3. Consideration of methods of improvement or new methods
4. Determining the best new method
5. Program for putting new method into practice

One of the biggest problems in a multiple agenda conference is that of covering all the matters on the agenda. In conference A, the agenda consists of one major item that needs to be communicated to the group and explained, that of new company policy on reporting to work. This might be explained and made clear in a minimum amount of time, but questions and problems might come up regarding putting the policy into practice that were not anticipated. If these take longer than planned by the conference leader, he will have to decide whether to take the extra time or move on to other items on the agenda. In this instance, it is probably more important to discuss this fully and postpone items 2 and 3, which are presumably not urgent and could be taken up at a later meeting. In conference B, the chances are that it would be desirable to cover all the items on the agenda at least briefly, for in this kind of a meeting it is important to bring the whole picture before the group. If some of the training programs under consideration need more discussion to work out problems and plans, these will undoubtedly be carried over until another meeting. Sometimes it is better to do this than to extend the time of the present meeting beyond schedule. *Conference members have a right to plan for being released from the conference at the scheduled time.*

In conference C, the matter under discussion is one major problem involving the production efficiency of the conference group itself. There has apparently been excessive damage to merchandise because of faults in the present packaging methods. It behooves this group to devote as much time as needed to the solution of this problem before adjourning the conference, for this is vital to the successful accomplishment of the work objective.

5. *Send notice to all who attend.* All too frequently a conference is called at the last minute while secretaries make frantic attempts to telephone all persons who are to attend. Disgruntled conferees come into the conference room in an uncooperative mood and resenting the fact that their workday has been broken up. Among

those who might be interested there is a feeling of uncertainty and wonder as to what the meeting is all about. This may be necessary in an emergency, but most conferences are not emergencies and there is little excuse for not sending notice sufficiently in advance of the meeting so that members can prepare for it. Such a notice should contain all necessary information about the conference and should include a copy of the agenda, or at least an indication of the purpose and subject of the meeting, in a form similar to this:

CONFERENCE NOTICE

To: _____

Please plan to attend a conference of _____

(name of group)

Place: _____

Time: _____

Purpose: _____

Persons attending: _____

(list names if small group)

Be prepared to talk on: _____

Please notify me if you cannot attend or if you have any suggestions for the agenda of the conference.

_____

Chairman (or job title)

A copy of the agenda is attached.

This notice suggests that a member might be told in advance that he should come prepared to talk on a particular topic. This would be done where the member's experience or knowledge would bring desirable information before the group, perhaps as background for discussion. A member also appreciates knowing in advance the names of the other conferees so that he can better prepare for his participation. If these can be listed in the conference notice, it is usually appreciated.

A shorter form, combining notice and agenda, is shown on the following page.

CONFERENCE NOTICE AND AGENDA

To:

You are invited to attend a conference of the _____

Time: Place:

The following matters will be discussed:

1.
2.
3.

Please be prepared to discuss these subjects.

I would appreciate your notifying me if you cannot attend.

_____
Chairman (or job title)

6. *Arrange facilities.* This simple suggestion stated another way means to have *everything* needed for a good conference arranged for and at hand *before the meeting starts.* And this would include items as big as the room itself down to a piece of chalk at the blackboard. Although the facilities for a conference will vary, they would usually include these:

• A pleasant, well-lighted room
• An appropriate arrangement of tables and chairs
• Name cards, pads, pencils, and other items at each place
• Visual aids or audio-visual equipment as needed
• Small speaker's stand if needed

Good conference rooms, properly equipped, are as essential to the successful operation of a business as machines that turn out the product. If an organization has such rooms available, a chairman calling a conference has very little to do in getting ready for his meeting. He must be sure that he has engaged a room from the person who is in charge of scheduling. All too frequently he assumes this has been done or that it is not necessary, only to go into the room at the scheduled time to find another group using it. A central point of record-keeping, with a specific person in charge of scheduling, will facilitate the making of arrangements.

The requirements for a pleasant conference room can vary considerably if one considers minimum to maximum extremes. A well-lighted, comfortably heated room with soft green walls, soft carpet, drapes, large mahogany tables, leather upholstered swivel chairs for conferees, and similar minor appointments might contribute to the success of the conference. Yet in another situation such a room could be out of place. Conferees generally like to feel "comfortable" in the room, in the same sense that they feel it approximates the surroundings and facilities they are used to in their own offices. One who sits at a swivel chair and is used to this in his work place will feel most at home in a swivel chair at a conference, or at least a chair with arms. The same could be said of a rug on the floor. Although we can make unreasonable demands for conference facilities, anyone in an organization who can influence the procuring of more comfortable conference surroundings will take an important step toward having more successful conferences.

The most *appropriate arrangement* of tables and chairs should be considered in relation to the particular group. Conferences are most successful when all members see each other face to face. If the group is small enough, this can best be accomplished at a round table which induces informality and tends to bring the leader into the group itself. The square or oblong table arrangement may be just as satisfactory. Depending on the size of the group, one large table (or tables) may accommodate up to twenty in a face-to-face seating arrangement. Diagrams A and B in Fig. 5-1 show such arrangements. In a larger group, the U arrangement of tables is next desirable, with members seated opposite each other on both sides of both rows of tables. If the room is large enough and there are sufficient tables, a square arrangement may be used, seating members only on the outside of the square. These arrangements are shown in diagrams C and D.

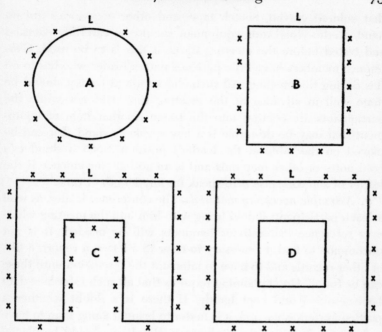

Fig. 5-1 Conference seating arrangements.

Sometimes small things can contribute to the discomfort of conferees and thus to the success or failure of the meeting. Ash trays should be within reach of everyone, and note-taking facilities should be at each place. In situations where the members are not known to each other, name cards should be made, or a folded cardboard can be used on which each person may print his name. If this is done on both sides, persons at both ends of the table will be able to see the name.

The conference room should be equipped with a blackboard or chart easel, or both. These should be placed properly in the front of the room, within sight of all members. If charts are to be developed during the conference, it is well to check and be sure that colored crayon, Scotch tape, and other accessories are on hand. Audio-visual aids equipment should be carefully checked and tested before the meeting starts, if this is to be used. Conference members have little patience with a leader who has to do this during the meeting. All such checking and testing should be done well in advance of the meeting time and not while the participants are coming into the room. Another item of equipment that may be desirable is a low speaker's stand that can be placed on the table at the leader's position. Such a stand can hold notes or other materials and is an added convenience if the leader or someone else is to speak for any length of time.

7. *Assemble necessary materials.* The conference leader, as well as each participant, should bring with him into the meeting whatever reference materials or handouts will be needed. It is not uncommon to find it necessary to refer to a letter, a report, a file, or other records and to have to interrupt the discussion until these can be found. Good planning requires that all such reference data be assembled and kept handy. If there is a doubt whether a particular item is needed, it is better to bring it along than to have to hunt for it during the conference. Handouts should be placed on the table near the leader, or in a convenient place, in sufficient quantity to distribute at the appropriate time.

8. *Prepare an outline for leading the discussion.* This is the most specific and important step in conference planning bearing on the actual leadership of the conference. The conference outline is the leader's plan and guide which he will use for carrying out the objective of the conference while guiding it through a logical sequence.

The conference outline differs from the agenda in that it is a more complete and detailed plan of the conference from beginning to end and is *solely for the use of the leader.* It shows a breakdown of all the subjects on the agenda, the continuity of the main points and questions that should be taken up under each subject, and the methods and techniques to be used during each phase of the discussion. A good form is to develop the outline on the right side of a page, using the left side to indicate the methods and special tools or techniques. If the conference has two major subjects, one informational in nature and the other problem-solving, a separate outline for each might be prepared.

The outline is of course a *flexible* guide which represents the leader's best judgment *before* the meeting as to how the discussion should be conducted. He should be ready to make adjustments and changes as the meeting progresses, and he should never regard the outline as a rigid pattern to be followed exactly. Keeping in mind the basic patterns of conference discussion, the leader's outline for conference agenda A shown above would look something like this:

CONFERENCE LEADER'S OUTLINE

Regular staff meeting.
Purpose: To explain new company policy on reporting to work, and to discuss problems of supervision.

TIME	METHOD AND TECHNIQUES	SUBJECTS
2:00 P.M.	Put members at ease Develop interest	I. Opening remarks and greeting A. Statement of purpose B. Subjects to be taken up

	First subject
	
	Use chart 1
	Use chart 2
	Handout of printed policy
	
	Ask QUESTIONS
	
	Put possible solutions on
	   BOARD
	Explain action
	
	TRANSITION to next subject
		II. Explanation of new policy on reporting to work
		A. Features of old policy
		B. Features of new policy
		C. Discuss printed policy
		   Answer questions
		D. PROBLEMS under new policy?
		   1. What problems?
		   2. Possible solutions?
		   3. Best solution?
		   4. ACTION to be taken?

TIME	METHOD AND TECHNIQUES	SUBJECTS
3:00	*Second subject*	III. Problem of cooperation with other departments
		A. Problem analysis
	Ask questions	1. Is there a problem?
		2. How serious is it?
	Assemble all the FACTS	3. What examples are there?
		4. Who? What? When? How? Where?
	Get suggestions from group	B. What are the possible solutions?
	Some suggestions to consider	1. Exchange visits with other departments?
	Put suggestions on BOARD	2. Have other department supervisors explain operations at our staff meetings?
		3. Other proposals?
	EVALUATE each solution	C. Which of these seems best?
		1. Will it work?
		2. Any new evils?
	Arrive at best solution	D. What specific recommendations should we make?
	Leave decision up to GROUP	E. What action should we take?
3:30	TRANSITION to next subject	IV. Problem of supervisors giving personal advice to workers
	BASIC QUESTION	A. Should a supervisor give advice to workers on personal matters?
	Use CASE A and B	1. Under what conditions?
	Analyze cases	2. What is wrong with this?

TIME	METHOD AND TECHNIQUES	SUBJECTS
		3. How could it have been handled better?
	Put suggestions for standards on BOARD	B. Can we arrive at a set of standards for doing this?
	TIME MAY NOT PERMIT FINISHING AT THIS MEETING. CARRY OVER TO NEXT MEETING.	
4:00		Closing remarks and summary
	ADJOURN on time	A. Announcements
		B. Plan for next meeting

The leader may also want to prepare an *outline of his introductory remarks* if these are to be extended very much. Or if he is to talk at some length in presenting and explaining information to the group, such as in point II of the above outline, these remarks should be prepared in fuller outline form prior to the meeting. They should also be practiced for timing to insure that this talk is not too long in relation to the group participation. Opening remarks, or an informative talk early in the meeting, should not become long-winded, for as soon as the group gets the impression that the leader is doing all the talking, it is much harder to get them to participate.

In planning the outline and the methods he will use to get maximum understanding and participation, the leader should also *plan the material he will put on the blackboard or chart* as the meeting progresses. Too often when this is done on an impromptu basis, the material has no organization or is not neat or the leader finds he does not have enough room for it. Of course whatever he plans in advance must be tentative and subject to wide variation as the group makes suggestions, but the planning is helpful nevertheless. At different stages of the conference, the leader might list the objective and main points of the conference, aspects

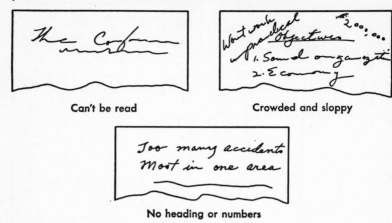

Fig. 5-2   How *not* to put material on blackboard or chart.

of the problem, causes of the problem, suggested solutions, pros and cons on specific solutions, action steps to be taken, or other lists of items. There is no one way to do this, and the diagrams of Fig. 5-3 are only suggested forms. If a chart easel is used, each list can be on a separate chart and hung up before the group as the meeting progresses. This is an aspect of leadership discussed further in Chap. 6.

Prepared charts, made in advance of the meeting, should also be considered, particularly when the leader has graphic material, data, or diagrams that should be before the group and can be prepared most attractively in a room where facilities are available. The time for the display of these should be carefully considered and planned.

9. *Prepare for participation.* Most of our suggestions for preparation are for the leader, and it is true that he has the greatest responsibility for the success of the conference, particularly as this success may stem from planning. But participants far too frequently make no preparation at all, and they make the mistake of just walking into the meeting "cold." *A good participant must anticipate and plan for his participation,* going through somewhat the same steps as the conference leader and relating them to his

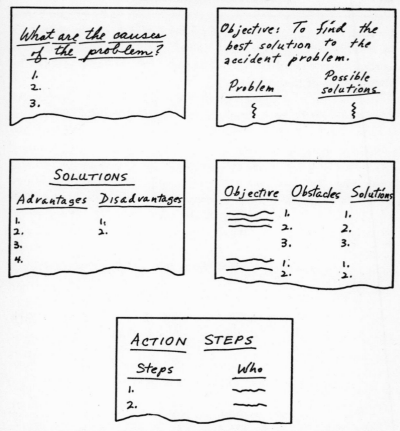

Fig. 5-3 Suggested forms for putting material on board or charts.

role as a member of the group. He should study the agenda, noting carefully the objectives to be accomplished and the subjects to be taken up. He should think through these subjects in terms of his own information and experience with them and any suggestions or convictions he may have on courses of action. If these are strong, he should determine to be open-minded as he listens to others in the group. Then he should go over the membership in the group, thinking through the relationship of other participants to his own position. He should look through his own materials and see whether he might have some data or items that he should bring into the meeting for reference or to help him in making certain points that he wants to contribute. His own participation should be related to that of others and adapted to the progress of the meeting.

10. *Plan for making a report of the results.* Some system should be established for recording and reporting the results of the conference, and this should not be left to memory or random impromptu method. It is therefore a part of conference planning, since the leader must insure that this will be done before the conference starts. In staff conferences and other types of meetings in an organization, a report is transmitted to the next higher level of management, usually the leader's superior. If a conference program is being coordinated by the personnel or training department, a copy of the report should be sent there. The group members may also decide in favor of each receiving a copy of the report.

It is the leader's responsibility to see that the report is made, although he may designate a member of the group as recorder or observer. Some suggestions for the report are:

• The date, time, and place of the meeting should be shown.
• Names of persons in attendance should be listed (if not too long).
• Major subjects discussed and action decided upon should be stated. This should be brief, and the nature of the discussion should not be included. Recommendations and suggestions should stand out clearly at the end of the report.

CONFERENCE REPORT FORM

Organization or work unit ————————————
Date and place held ————————————
Called by ————————————
Persons present ————————————
Purpose of conference ————————————
Subjects discussed ————————————

Actions and recommendations _____

General comment _____

Reported by _____

Conclusion

Conference planning cannot be taken lightly. Most breakdowns that occur within the conference itself can be attributed to some failure in the planning stage. A good way to insure that you have planned well and completely is to use a check list such as this each time you are responsible for calling and leading a conference.

CONFERENCE PLANNING CHECK LIST

1. Have I determined the exact PURPOSE of the meeting? _____
2. Have all PARTICIPANTS been considered? _____
   * Special guests or speakers? _____
   * Has NOTICE been sent to all? _____
3. Has complete GROUP ANALYSIS been made? _____
   * Knowledge and experience? _____
   * Attitudes and prejudices? _____
   * Silent and talkative? _____
4. Has AGENDA been prepared? _____
   * Have I consulted with participants? _____
   * Has copy been sent to each? _____
   * Possible hidden agendas considered? _____
5. Have FACILITIES been arranged? _____
   * Room engaged? _____
   * Proper table and chair arrangement? _____
   * Blackboard, chart easel, chalk, crayons, pointer, speaker's stand, pads, pencils, name cards? _____
   * Audio-visual equipment checked? _____
6. Do I have all reference MATERIALS at hand? _____
7. Have I prepared an OUTLINE of the discussion? _____
   * Does it show complete plan? _____
   * Questions and special methods? _____
   * Introductory remarks prepared? _____
   * Considered timing and transitions? _____
8. Have I planned for a REPORT? _____
   * Asked someone to help with this? _____
   * Determined who will receive it? _____

APPLYING THIS CHAPTER

1. Prepare an agenda for a conference based on a problem in your work scene. Make up an appropriate notice and a list of all persons to whom the notice and agenda will be sent.
2. At this same conference, might you have some information to tell the group on another subject? How and at what time will you work this into the agenda? Develop a complete outline from the agenda, showing how you plan to lead the entire conference.
3. Think of some examples of meetings you attended where planning and preparing might have avoided difficulties.
4. Observe in a conference you attend or lead the extent to which the prepared outline was followed or revised or amended as the discussion unfolded.
5. What do you feel is the ideal physical arrangement for a business conference?
6. Have you ever been drawn into a conference without sufficient notice, causing you to be a dissatisfied participant? How does this affect your own participation and that of other members?

III

CONFERENCE AND DISCUSSION IN ACTION

As they walk into the conference room, both leader and participant should be equipped with the proper attitudes, and the necessary tools, methods, and techniques for carrying out their respective jobs. Leading a successful conference is not a job to be taken lightly. The leader must understand his role, his relation to the group, and the leadership qualities and tools he must have. The participant must understand himself and the others in the group, and he must make use of the best methods of participation. The leader and the total group must understand methods of reaching decisions and of evaluating what they have done in the conference room.

CHAPTER 6

Leadership

LEADERSHIP is a rare combination of attitude, personal qualities, and the use of tools and methods that add up to techniques. Although the role of the leader is extremely important to the successful conference, a good meeting is not a one-man show, but rather it is the entire group working together. This is why the good leader will approach his job with a broad understanding of the total group and the people in it and of the principles of group interaction and human relations, not just with a bag of tricks and techniques that someone told him would be the exact answer to every problem of leadership. There are no such tricks, and there is no panacea for effective leadership of discussion. Yet there are certain basic attitudes, relationships, qualities, and tools which add up to good leadership. This chapter will discuss the total job of leadership as we develop these.

We shall be using the terms "conference leader" and "conference leadership," since leadership is our primary concern at this point.[1] Most of what we say in this chapter would apply to discussion leadership of any kind of meeting.

The Leader's Attitude

The conference is basically a *cooperative* medium. This determines the basic attitude with which you approach your job as

[1] The more specific application of leadership principles and methods to public discussion situations is discussed in Chap. 11.

leader: it must be one of getting as much out of your group as possible, with a minimum of control and participation on your part. Leadership is a philosophy, carrying over into the conference room the leader's general habits of life in relation to other people. The more he has developed an attitude of understanding, respecting, and liking others, the better he will be inclined to realize that a conference is *their* meeting and not his, except in situations where he has to be in control because of the peculiar nature of the meeting's objective.

We speak of this attitude as being **group-centered** rather than self-centered, which is the natural tendency of most of us. Actually all of the principles and tools we take up in this chapter, as well as the qualities we look for in a good conference leader, are selected because they help in some way to contribute toward the objective of group-mindedness and group participation rather than leader dominance and control. Group members are there to contribute, and it is up to you to give them maximum opportunities consistent with the purpose of the meeting. If it is a true problem-solving meeting, let it be so by putting the discussion and ultimate solution in their hands.

The word "permissive" is used a great deal today to describe the atmosphere the conference leader should try to establish in relation to his group's feeling that they are free to contribute. If every member of a group feels at all times that he can say whatever he thinks and not be criticized by the leader (members must of course expect others in the group possibly to disagree), the leader has probably succeeded in removing his own personality and opinion from the control of thought and expression of others. In order to do this in a problem-solving conference, he must show at all times that he is open-minded, quite impartial, and understanding of all that others say. This requires almost complete absence of comment on the remarks of participants which in any way would reveal the leader's agreement or disagreement, or even whether he likes the person as an individual. This principle should also be emphasized in respect to the caution against showing that any special interest is at stake or any particular individual in the group is favored.

Proper attitude, then, includes open-mindedness, objectivity, tolerance, and understanding on your part. It stems from a philosophy of wanting to develop a democratic group, of recognizing the value of information and judgments that rest within the group members, and of wanting to give all a feeling of participation in helping you make the best decisions possible for them. The conference leader with this kind of attitude is one who thinks in terms of *people* who make up the group.

The Leader's Qualities

When we add up all the qualities that make for a good conference leader, we can start with the philosopher's interpretation of the "good man" who acquires the tools of discussion leading. Quintilian's definition of the good speaker as a good man who is skilled in speaking is probably even more appropriate to describe the conference leader, for his qualities of goodness as a person stand out more sharply than those of the public speaker, who is not as intimately related to the people about him. So we could say that if you would be a good conference leader, you should first become a totally good person and stop right here. But we can list some of the more specific qualities that are helpful to the leader of a group:

Poise	Tact
Understanding and	Sense of humor
liking others	Intelligence
Sensitivity	Animation
Impartiality	Speaking and listening

In discussing these qualities, we must keep in mind that they add up to the "ideal" leader who is in a position where he gives (or should give) the most possible deference to the group and the individuals in it both in the conduct of the conference and the conclusion reached. We shall see in our next section that it is not always possible for him to do this, yet the qualities we have listed should still be cultivated.

• *Poise* is that somewhat mysterious quality which we say a person has when we see him, but we are hard put to describe what we mean. It involves personal bearing, even to the inclusion of such physical things as posture, facial expression, and movement. One does not get poise by slouching in a chair, staring into space, or mumbling into his notes. Preparation also has a great deal to do with poise, for a confident person usually has poise—and confidence stems from feeling prepared. Many of the qualities discussed below also add up to poise.

• We have already commented on the importance of *understanding and liking others.* If you really enjoy being with and working with people, it usually shows up both in your manner and in the way you run a meeting. The leader who regards his conference members only as objects occupying seats simply goes through the mechanical motions of running a conference; he does not build a cooperative group of people. The student of human relations tries to understand why a certain member won't talk on a particular issue and why another gets emotionally aroused on another problem. You as a conference leader should study people in general and get to understand them, then apply some of the principles of analysis discussed in Chap. 3.

• *Sensitivity* comes from understanding and enjoying people, as well as analysis of the particular subject, problems, issues, and setting in which a discussion is taking place. A cold, aloof person is the opposite of a sensitive person. The quality of sensitivity enables you to be alert to understand remarks that are made in a discussion, how they affect others, and what you as leader can best do at the time.

• *Impartiality* is another word for open-mindedness and objectivity. This quality has already been stressed, particularly as it is needed in a problem-solving situation. We shall point out in the following section some situations where the conference leader cannot be completely impartial, but this makes it no less important that you develop this quality for your best total development as a leader. It is largely a matter of analyzing the purpose, problems, and issues that are likely to come into a discussion and your own feelings and convictions in relation to them. In this way you can determine "danger spots" that might occur in your leadership and what you can do to avoid them. Or you can determine that in a given case you must set the policy or explain the information yourself and thus frankly indicate to the group why you cannot leave the matter to them.

• *Tact* is another little word that we can usually recognize in people but find hard to define. It is probably the basic quality that contains all the others, for tact has to do with the total manner we show in our relations with other people. It is also described as "saying the right thing at the right time in the right way," but this doesn't help us much, since this would embody all the principles of effective communication with others. Surely if one is understanding, sensitive, and impartial, he will be tactful. Respect for the feelings, position, and judgment of others is also required.

• To have a *sense of humor* does not require that you develop ability as a comedian or master of ceremonies, or that you build up a large repertoire of jokes. It is a quality of not taking too seriously what someone has said or not taking offense too readily, of turning a tense situation into a pleasant one by a light and appropriate remark, and of otherwise indicating that you are a pleasant person to be around. Sometimes having a few stories or jokes at hand and using one at a proper time may be advisable, but having a sense of humor does not necessarily imply this. Actually this quality is part of a philosophy of life. The truly effective leader will know when he can make light of a situation as well as when it would be fatal to do so. Showing a pleasant facial expression and smile frequently helps a great deal.

• One of Webster's definitions of *intelligence* is "the power of meeting any situation ... successfully by proper behavior adjustments; also the ability to apprehend the interrelationships of presented facts in such a way as to guide action towards a desired goal." This says almost everything we would want to say in applying the quality of intelligence to discussion. The intelligent discussion leader has made thorough preparation which included a logical analysis of the subject. He applies his ability to reason and think through a situation as the discussion unfolds, and he makes the right decisions as to leadership methods and tools at every point. The latter point is extremely important because of the tendency of many conference leaders to employ a certain tool or method blindly just because some "expert" advanced it as a panacea for effective leadership. There is no one tool that is thus valuable at all times, and it does take intelligence and judgment on the part of the leader to decide his leadership methods in a given instance.

• *Animation* means being alive and enthusiastic in what you are doing. All we need say here is that enthusiasm is contagious, and your group will soon sense whether you are enjoying what you are doing or just regarding it as a chore. The leader who starts his meeting with "Well, it's our regular meeting day again. These conferences sure do come up on us. I don't have anything much to take up today . . . do you?" will find about as much enthusiasm in his group as his words and manner convey.

• We have emphasized the importance of good *speaking and listening* in many parts of this book, and they are no less important as qualities of the conference leader. Most of the principles of leadership point in the direction of minimum *amount* of speaking by the leader, which would indicate that he does much more listening than speaking and therefore should develop this quality more. This is probably true, yet even in the most permissive problem-solving conference, where he gives the group complete control of the discussion and the outcome, the leader's minimum contributions as a speaker should be spoken well. Some of the pitfalls will serve to emphasize the characteristics of good speaking we want to see. Because he is seated and generally in a conversational rather than a public speaking manner, the leader is inclined to speak too low for all to hear him, to mumble indistinctly, to look at the table rather than the group, to favor a few persons either seated near him or those he likes by looking at them all the time, to slouch in the chair, to lean the chin on a hand, to hold a hand over the mouth, to play with an object, to make too frequent use of notes, to talk into the blackboard or chart if he is using one, to shout excitedly out of proportion to the size of the room or group, to have incoherent organization of his ideas, to develop his ideas uninterestingly and only with vague generalities, to use no transitions or summaries, and to speak without a purpose. It would be hard to find all these faults in any one person, and their opposites are too frequently not found.

Some *listening faults* should also be avoided, such as refusing to listen to certain people we don't like, "daydreaming" about other things, not looking at the speaker, being too self-centered, listening to refute rather than to understand, allowing prejudices to intervene, failing to understand the speaker's position, and others. The conference leader's listening must be sympathetic, alert, active, and understanding. He must follow closely the trend of the discussion so that he knows at all times what is happening in the group, who might best be recognized next, how to resolve tension and conflict, when to make transitions, and how to summarize, along with many other reasons. Alert listening also enables the leader to spot talkative and silent members.

The Leader-Group Relationship

The leader-group relationship is the key to the total conference process. Despite what we say about the qualities and skills of the ideal conference leader and our regard for him as a pleasant guide who sits back and lets the group take over with a maximum amount of participation on their part, we know that in many situations this is not the case. We often do not have ideal leadership, even though we strive for it. But one of the real mistakes we make when we observe a leader who appears to be far from ideal is to condemn him as a bad leader.

Most discussion situations call for a leader and a group, each of which has a part to play in the ultimate outcome. The part each plays depends not only on what kind of people they are and what qualities they possess, *but the type of meeting and the purpose to be accomplished.* And herein lie some special problems of the leader-group relationship which are as important to understand as any other principles and methods in this book.

Actually, the proper management of a conference by the leader does not follow from a rigid mold of what makes the good leader in a general sense. It follows rather from a resourceful leader who has learned both the skills and methods of leadership and how to apply them *in the particular conference.* In other words, different conferences call for different kinds and methods of leadership. This is best illustrated in the diagram which shows the relationship between the leader and the group in regard to the amount of control each exercises in the outcome (and hence in the relative amount of participation of each) in accomplishing different kinds of conference objectives.

One of the problems of defining the leader's role and determining his degree of control over the outcome of a meeting is that we have developed a rather broad definition and usage of the word "conference" to include all types of meetings ranging from pure information-giving to pure problem-solving. Then we correspondingly attach to each the same requirements and characteristics of leadership. Some suggest solving this problem by not calling the purely information-giving meeting a conference, but this semantic shift of definition is not of much practical value. We have become far too much accustomed to using the label for all kinds of meetings, particularly in a business organization, and when we are asked to attend a "conference," we usually picture our own stereotyped definition.

We must recognize this wide range of conference objectives in planning how we will lead a particular meeting (or conference)

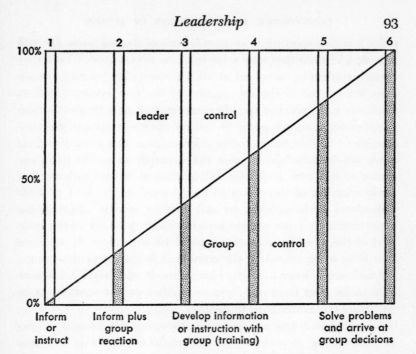

Fig. 6-1 Relationship of leader and group control of outcome, depending on nature and objective of meeting. (Adapted from E. S. Hannaford, *Conference Leadership in Business and Industry*, p. 8, McGraw-Hill Book Company, Inc., New York, 1945.)

and to what extent we can allow for or encourage group participation and control over the outcome. For all practical purposes, we must realize that there are situations within the average organization which call for variety and resourcefulness in the way conferences are conducted. If we look at a series of weekly meetings of the average supervisor with his subordinates, we can see how this comes about.

The company top management has just negotiated a new contract with the union. At this particular weekly conference the supervisor's job is to explain the contract and how it will affect the work group. He masters this information and is the only one in the group who has it. Obviously, he will do most of the talking at this meeting, and he will control the outcome. He will answer questions that may arise from his explanation. There may be no problem to be solved at all. Or there may be minor problems arising out of the explanation of the new contract and its application. In another weekly conference, a new production demand of top management may call for the entire time of the conference to be devoted to the problem of how this group can best work out its schedule to meet the demands of production. The leader in this case wants the full participation and judgment of every member of the group to help formulate the best possible procedures and methods. In still another weekly meeting, the supervisor may have certain information to pass on in the early part of the meeting; then there might be several small problems that have to be solved by the combined judgment of the group.[2] He will surely have to change his methods and "style" of leadership as he goes from one item to another on the agenda, as he will from one conference to another.

The kind and type of leadership, then, are determined at least in part by the objective to be accomplished, and this will have a direct bearing on the kind and amount of group participation. We can best see the difference by showing three patterns of group participation resulting from three kinds of leadership (recognizing, of course, that there are many degrees in between).

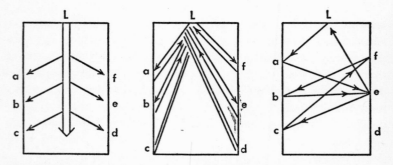

Fig. 6-2 Types of leader control affecting participation. Extreme, strong, and minimum control (left to right).

[2] See sample agendas in Chap. 5.

The leader who exercises extreme control may go so far as not to conduct a conference at all. He is then referred to as the "autocratic" or "dogmatic" leader who does all the talking and insists on imposing his will on the group. These terms applied to him necessarily imply wrongdoing, as far as our usual concepts of the good leader are concerned. Yet this kind of leadership, if we apply terms such as "lecturer" or "speaker," may be perfectly commendable in the particular meeting wherein the objective is best accomplished by talking to the group. We must recognize that such a relationship between the leader and the group is perfectly justified where he is in complete command of the facts or information and calls the group together to inform them, as in certain instructional or training conferences.

The second pattern of relationship causes more difficulty, for it usually stems from a leader who has called the group together presumably to "talk things over," yet insists on keeping the entire exchange between himself and members. This leader is always in the picture, commenting after each remark of a member and probably making use of the direct question to specific members to induce remarks rather than allow free participation. Either he is unskilled in the methods for bringing about total group participation, or he is afraid to allow the group to take over the discussion and perhaps control the outcome.

The third pattern is what most of us like to feel is the ideal type of exchange and participation by the members, with the least possible guidance and control by the leader. This is the true problem-solving situation, where both leader and group know that the outcome is in the hands of the group and the ultimate decisions will be theirs. This is the objective that most of the tools and methods of leadership discussed later in this chapter are designed to produce. Such leadership tends to be nondirective and laissez-faire.

The *length* of the conference may also be a determining factor in the amount of participation a leader can allow the group. Although we do not like to have to admit this, the realism of many practical business situations imposes a time limitation which the conference leader must recognize. We have already agreed that the conference is a time-consuming medium, and one of the leader's responsibilities is to see that the maximum is accomplished in the time available. In the case of a particular policy to be established by top management, each supervisor is asked to report the decision and recommendations of his group on a certain afternoon, so that top management can take these into consideration in establishing company policy. It is the sort of problem that could best be solved in several meetings, over a period of days, but both leader and group have to accept the exigencies of the situation and take this into account in the amount of participation possible.

The information-developmental conference, which is the typical training or instructional conference, also requires certain controls by the leader in order to insure the outcome required. In some training conferences, for example, in human relations training where the group is discussing a case, the leader can let the group go in a completely permissive manner to draw conclusions and principles from the case. However, where he is in command of the principles or facts he wishes the group to know and learn from the discussion, he must exercise a certain amount of control in order to insure that these are properly before the group.

It is therefore not a simple matter to generalize and say that the best conferences come about when the leader resigns to a position where he is in least possible control (or, as some suggest, where he is actually absorbed into the group in favor of members assuming leadership duties, which we discuss more under leaderless discussion later in this chapter). The hard facts of a business conference do not always permit the luxury of free discussion. In industrial and military organizations, decisions sometimes must be left to the person to whom the responsibility for them has been assigned, and this is frequently the conference leader. We thus see that a number of factors add up to determine the leader-group relationship in regard to control and participation and the type, style, and quality of leadership: the kind of person the leader is, the qualities of leadership he possesses, the objective of the particular conference, the time factor, and the kind of group.

When the leader tends to exercise control over the outcome, and hence over the discussion itself, we use the terms "restricted" or "closely shaped" to describe the type of leadership. When the group is given complete freedom to shape the outcome, we use the terms "free" and "pure" to describe the total conference activity. In the former, the leader has probably predetermined to some extent the outcome desired in advance of the meeting. If this is so, he should be careful not to give the impression to the group that the outcome is in their hands, for they will soon sense the artificiality of their discussion.

We might summarize the characteristics of leader and group control as they compare in the two major types of conference objectives:

CHARACTERISTICS OF LEADER–GROUP CONTROL

IN INFORMATIONAL-INSTRUCTIONAL CONFERENCES	IN PROBLEM-SOLVING CONFERENCES
Leader control dominant	Group control dominant
Tend to be restricted and closely shaped	Tend to be free, pure, and permissive
Leader tends to make decisions	Group tends to make decisions

The Leader's Responsibilities

As we add up and try to define through research and practice the many duties and responsibilities of the conference leader, we realize more and more that the job is a difficult one and that we do not often find the perfect leader. Some have observed that we should not expect one person to do all that is required, and that he should be relieved of some responsibilities by an assistant leader or that there should be less leadership by one and more assumption of leadership duties by group members. The extreme of this suggestion is leaderless discussion. The Laboratory of Social Relations at Harvard University,[3] after much research on leadership, concluded that most conferences do have two leaders: the actual leader or "task leader," who appears to be the leader and who called the meeting, and the "social leader," who emerges from the group as the best liked of its members. Such a person may be the most talkative or the most congenial and is one whom the group has grown to respect, and it is generally advised that the actual leader accept him as a helper and integrate his leadership with his own.

When such a person *emerges as a leader* because of the weak leadership of the actual leader, interesting reactions may develop. There is a tendency for group members to assume leadership functions from a weak leader. If this is done in the absence of the leader doing them, the group usually approves. However, when members take over such functions that are already being well executed by the conference leader, there tends to be a resentment in such groups against these members.

Leaderless discussion is an outgrowth of the feeling that a group can achieve maximum results with the least possible amount of leadership. Hence the completely permissive and free atmosphere suggested by some of the leaders in the Group Dynamics movement can be achieved most fully with no leader at all. The suggestion is that the group sit around a table without a leader and that the leadership responsibilities will be taken over from time to time by different members. The advocates of this procedure suggest it also because of the complexities of the leader's job; that is, since it is so difficult to get good leaders, we should have no leaders at all. There are of course very few situations in which leaderless discussion would be practical, except perhaps in extremely informal parlor conversations where the group has no particular objective to accomplish. Such discussion is apt to be discursive, disorganized, and unrealistic for any kind

[3] Robert F. Bales, "How People Interact in Conferences," *Scientific American*, vol. 192, March, 1955.

of a meeting with a purpose. There is also the danger that the emergent leadership that would result may create rivalries for the leader position among the strong members of the group.

The Conference Research Project at the University of Michigan came to some interesting conclusions regarding strong and weak leadership.[4] They concluded that a strong, positive leader who expressed himself with conviction and emphasis tended to induce strong and positive contributions from the group. Conversely, they concluded that the weak or submissive leader drew less positive contributions. There is an implication of certain values from dominant leadership if it can be said that this tends to keep group activity in a positive rather than a negative direction.

One of the real difficulties, however, is in the terms we use to define different characteristics of leadership, terms meaning different things to different people. When we speak of a "strong" leader, this may imply one who dominates or who is autocratic, these being generally considered as negative qualities. Then again, a "strong" leader may be one who exercises just the right amount of control in keeping with the meeting's objective, while possessing none of the negative qualities of the autocratic leader. Another interpretation is the use of the word "strong" as a synonym for "good" leadership, and the word "weak" as a synonym for "bad" leadership. Yet we use the term "weak" also to describe the leader who sits back and lets the group have an uncontrolled, permissive, and free atmosphere which is what we sometimes say is an ideal of "pure" conference.

In listing the leader's specific responsibilities in running a conference, we must keep these considerations in mind.

LEADER'S RESPONSIBILITIES

Accomplish the purpose of the meeting
Start and keep discussion organized

[4] Roger W. Heyns, "Effects of Variation in Leadership on Participant Behavior in Group Discussions," Conference Research Project, Ann Arbor, Mich., 1948 (mimeographed release).

Stimulate, guide, and control discussion
Make decisions
Keep records

• We can theorize and philosophize at length about the leader, yet we can never lose sight of the fact that his primary responsibility is to *accomplish the purpose of the meeting*. All his plans prior to the meeting, and all the tools and methods he employs in leading it, are to meet this responsibility. This does not say that the end justifies the means, for we are going to some length to suggest and explain the various means he can employ, but when the conference is over, he must be able to say that it did achieve its purpose.

• Probably the most important responsibility toward gaining the conference purpose is that of *keeping the discussion organized*. Discussion that gets discursive, off the track, down side alleys, and into meaningless arguments is not likely to contribute toward the purpose of the meeting. That is why the leader must keep his eye on the agenda and the clock while he employs all the best tools and exhibits the best qualities of leadership that he can muster in the given case.

The *way he gets started* and the tone he sets at the outset will have a lasting effect throughout the conference. If there's a problem to be solved, he should indicate this to the group and the extent to which their judgment is wanted in finding a solution. He should be honest in explaining this as he discusses with them the reason for the meeting and what he feels the group should accomplish. He should avoid expressing his own views, such as "I've called you together to discuss a serious problem on which we want your advice. It is this ... Now I think there's only one way to solve it. I believe we have to ... This is a busy day and our time is short. What do you folks think?" He will get little response after this opening. Following the pattern of organization and the outline he has prepared, he should guide the group into the first point in the outline, perhaps using an overhead question, series of questions, case or example, or other method that will be most effective.

After the problem has been analyzed, he should make appropriate transition, posing for the group the specific issues or parts of the problem that seem most applicable in searching for possible solutions. These should be encouraged in a period of free contributions before they are analyzed and compared. He should then help the group discover the solution they first want to consider and the pattern of analysis most useful in this consideration (advantages-disadvantages, practical-impractical, etc.). As the group converges on a particular solution, he should attempt to anticipate consensus or disagreement. Then he should draw together with the group the steps in the action program to be recommended. These are some of the responsibilities he has in keeping the discussion organized, always making summaries that will help keep the main matters before the group at various stages of the discussion.

• *His job to stimulate, guide, and control discussion is the heart of his leadership in respect to the actual discussion process.* We discuss his tools and methods for doing this in the next section, and we can here summarize what this responsibility includes. The leader must *stimulate* the discussion with respect to the group as a whole, the individual members, and the particular point under consideration at a given time. He must *guide* the discussion through a systematic sequence, as we have just pointed out above. And he must *control*, with respect to the total group, individual members who talk either too much or too little, individual members who cause problems such as argument and tense situations, and the time factor in relation to accomplishing the conference objective.

Stimulating discussion comes from a variety of tools, including the leader's personal qualities and manner, questions, cases and examples, factual material, visual and audio-visual aids, role-playing, and the seating arrangement. Getting the silent member to talk is sometimes a most difficult job of the leader, as is getting a total group started in expressing itself. The latter is accomplished best at the outset by proper manner and tone, as has been pointed out, and by use of questions. If someone in a group does not voluntarily start the discussion after the leader has done what he can to set the stage, one point of view suggests that he simply wait until a member does speak up, however long this may take. Someone will eventually break the silence, and the total group will have been better off for the waiting period than if the leader himself decided to express a point of view. Fortunately, this kind of impasse does not often develop, but the leader should be prepared with a variety of tools in case the one first used does not work.

With regard to *individual silent members,* the leader should try to analyze the many reasons why one may not wish to talk in a particular group situation. Among these are natural shyness, a feeling of lack of involvement, lack of skill in speaking, emotional or physical fatigue, a too dominant leader, fear of other members who are too aggressive or in superior positions, lack of knowledge, lack of an opinion to express, or someone present who may be critical.[5] The good leader will try to put his finger on the reason and compensate for it perhaps by pointing up a phase of the problem that might interest this member or by calling for specific information he knows the member possesses. Direct questions to a silent member should be used with caution and only after the leader is fairly certain that he will respond.

The control of discussion with regard to the *total group* involves the leader's judgment as to how much and what kind of discussion he is getting from point to point and whether he should emphasize a new direction, stopping the discussion on the particular point in order to bring in other points and spreading the participation among the maximum number of persons. If one or a few members are monopolizing the discussion, he should suggest that others might wish to express themselves.

Some suggest that if the *too talkative member* can be spotted in advance, he should be placed in the so-called "blind" positions immediately to the right or left of the leader, where he will be less likely to be recognized. If there are several such persons, it is also best to seat them in different parts of the group so that there will not be an impression that much of the participation comes from one section of the group. Other means for controlling the talkative or argumentative member are to break in tactfully and ask others to comment on what he has said, use appropriate humor showing appreciation of his remarks, fail to recognize him by avoiding looking in his direction when questions are thrown to the group, keeping a record on participation of each person, and showing him after the meeting that he has talked way out of proportion to others. We should not assume, however, that the talkative member is necessarily not a good contributor or an asset to the group, as we shall see further in Chap. 7.

Heated argument can often be broken up by appropriate humor, by asking others to comment, and by pointing out that the argument has reached its maximum-value point to the group. The leader should be careful that he does not indicate his own opinion on the argument and does not take sides.

• *Making decisions,* or arriving at the results desired by the leader or the group, is basically a leadership responsibility in most conference situations. Even if the entire group judgment is to be the basis for the decision rather than the leader's, it is still usually his responsibility to see that the results of the discussion are clear and that they are transmitted to the proper persons. The process of decision-making is discussed fully in Chap. 8.

• *Keeping records* is also the responsibility of the leader, even though he should delegate the job to someone else such as a recorder, secretary, or observer. We have emphasized the method for making conference reports in Chap. 5, and we would again point out that a system should be established for keeping the reports of conferences together and in one place so that they are readily available.

Leadership Tools and Methods

We come now to discuss the specific tools and methods the leader may use in accomplishing the conference objective and carrying out his responsibilities. These are referred to throughout the pages of this book as the vital tools for carrying out the discussion process in leading, stimulating, guiding, and controlling group discussion in varied situations. The conference leader who learns their meaning and is able to use them in the appropriate instance will strengthen immeasurably his ability to lead a meeting.

> Questions
> Transitions and summaries
> Visual and audio-visual aids
>> Blackboard
>> Charts
>> Flannel board
>> Handouts
>> Demonstrations
>> Films, filmstrips, and records
> Cases and similar devices
>> Incidents
>> Role-playing
> Listening

QUESTIONS

Once you have reached the point where group participation is wanted, questions become the major tool for stimulating discussion, and they are probably the most used tool of the conference leader. There are two major types of questions: the *overhead* or *general* question, which is thrown out by the leader to the entire group, and the *direct* question, which is raised to a specific group member. The overhead question gets its name from the way it is used, since it is tossed out by the leader "over the heads" of the participants, with the thought that anyone might answer it and with the hope that someone will. It is the best way to stimulate total group thinking in that it alerts *everyone* to focus interest toward the point raised by the question, whereas the direct question tends to exclude the interest of the rest of the members who may sit back and withdraw, since they know the question is not for them.

Perhaps the biggest problem in using the overhead question is the fact that it may not bring a response at all. We pointed out above that sometimes the leader should just wait until someone does speak up. But it is usually better to have a series of follow-up questions ready that will narrow the point raised or make it more specific. An overhead question such as "What do you think?" is so broad that no one may respond to it. But it can be made more and more specific, such as "Who can give us some facts bearing on the problem?" "Just how serious is this problem?" "Whom does it affect?" "When did it start?" "What are the causes of the problem?" "How many accidents did we have last month?" "How many manhours were lost?" Members are quite likely to respond and volunteer information to these questions.

The direct question should be used with caution, for it puts a participant on the spot, and his failure to answer it causes embarrassment both to him and the leader. An alert leader who knows his members will be able to determine when he can draw on a specific individual. It is best to state the question, then single out the member to answer it, for in this way the entire group remains interested in the question more than it will when the leader starts with "Joe, can you tell us the number of accidents in your shop?"

Another caution is that of avoiding *leading questions*, which imply the answer the leader wants, for they both reveal that he is not impartial and indicate to the group that he really does not want their opinion after all. These are examples of leading questions: "Won't plan X be the best one for us after all?" "Isn't it a fact that this has already failed?" "You really don't think this will work, do you?" We also note that most leading questions require simply a yes-or-no answer and thus do not stimulate discussion.

Most questions are either *fact-finding* (information-seeking) or *opinion-seeking* in nature. In the early part of a problem-solving discussion, the questions should solicit as much factual information as possible, thus avoiding the use of opinion-seeking or value-judgment questions until later. It would also follow that in an information or instructional conference, more information-seeking questions would be used. Here are examples of each type:

Fact-finding and Information-seeking Questions

> *Where* did the problem start?
> *How* did it start? (Use what, when, how, who, where)
> *When* did it start?
> *Who* are the people responsible?
> *How much* does this cost us? Money? Manpower? Materials?
> *How many* people are affected?
> *What* are the causes?
> *Just what* does it add up to?

Before the period of discussion when opinion and judgment is asked for on various solutions, more general questions should be raised that will solicit possible solutions, during which opinion should be avoided. The proponents of creative and imaginative thinking and of brainstorming would encourage the group to suggest anything that comes to mind as a possible solution rather than one that appears logical or practical. At any rate, questions like these would be raised: "Can we now list some possible solutions?" "How would you suggest we solve the problem?"

Opinion-seeking and Value-judgment Questions

> Do you think this plan will solve the problem?
> Is this practical?
> What do you think of solution A? B? C?
> Will plan B remove the causes?
> In your judgment, what is the best plan?
> From your experience, will this work?

We have been discussing the use of questions raised by the leader to encourage participation from the group. He must also handle *questions raised by group members* which seek information or opinion. Such questions are usually aimed at the leader with the assumption that he will answer them. Actually, he should refrain from doing so as much as possible. There is a great temptation for the leader to answer these questions himself, for he is frequently in command of the facts needed, and he usually has an opinion. But this puts him in a position of "experting" and of dominating the discussion which could be contributed by members of the group. Such questions, then, should be *relayed* back to the group by the leader, in which he asks the question of the group as a whole in overhead fashion to see if someone will answer. Or he may ask it in direct fashion to an individual member. Or he may *reverse* the question back to the person who asked it, particularly if it seeks opinion or judgment. He might say, "That's an interesting question. What do you think of the suggestion yourself?" The skilled leader will continue to develop his ability to use questions as a basic leadership tool.

TRANSITIONS AND SUMMARIES

Appropriate transitions are one of the best tools for keeping discussion organized and for keeping everyone informed on the progress from point to point as well as on the particular point before them at a given time. The alert leader will sense when the group should move away from one point and on to the next. His remarks may utilize such language as "Now, let's turn to the next point," "Next we should consider . . . ," "With the analysis of the problem before us, let's think about some solutions," "Having discussed our first two points, let's look at the third." Transitions may also be facilitated by making internal summaries of what has been discussed, then indicating the next point. Frequent summaries throughout the discussion help achieve clear thinking and good organization. A summary at the start of the conference, indicating the main points and questions to be considered, also gives the group a preview of what is to come. Putting the main points and questions on the blackboard or on a chart will also add clarity. And the leader's responsibility for a final summary is obvious.

VISUAL AND AUDIO-VISUAL AIDS

The blackboard and the chart easel on which the leader can develop material as the conference progresses are the chief tools of visual aids in most meetings. In Chap. 5 we discussed the importance of planning the way in which this would be done and how it would appear. The *blackboard* is probably the most commonly used medium, since a portable board can be made available in most situations. The *chart easel* is gaining more acceptance, particularly in informational and training conferences, where the material is to be kept rather than erased and where it is desirable to keep the material before the group throughout the meeting or from one meeting to the next. A pad of white paper charts about 30 by 40 inches is placed on an easel, with the charts perforated at the top for ready removal. As one is filled, it is taken off and hung in a convenient position with an adhesive tape; then succeeding charts are developed. If this is not desired, each chart can be flipped back and retained on the easel for reference at a later point if necessary. Colored crayons can be used for variety and attractiveness.

A number of types of material can be developed in this way, including main points and subpoints, data and statistics, graphs and tables, and diagrams. One of the chief uses is to put points up on the chart or blackboard as they are contributed by group members. In doing this, the leader should be careful to include most of what is suggested and should be cautious in screening any of the suggestions. Members who feel their points are excluded are inclined to withdraw from further participation. The leader should get the feel of what the members and the group want him to put on the chart. Some suggest that this be done by someone other than the leader in order to free him for other leadership duties. However, this adds a mechanical factor which makes the procedure more stilted, and it takes the leader out of the center of involvement with the discussion.

Smaller easels and pads are also available to be placed on the table immediately to the right or left of the leader, who can record while remaining seated.

Prepared charts may also be used to stimulate discussion. The conference leader should decide whether certain material may be most effectively placed before the group on a chart prepared before the meeting. Complexity of the material may require this rather than rely on being able to develop it coherently in impromptu fashion during the meeting. Another consideration is whether it will be wise to have the group see the points on a chart all at one time. A technique to take care of this problem is to cover some of the lines of a chart with tape that can readily be peeled off as each point comes up for discussion. Still another technique gaining in use is the *flannel board,* which is usually on an easel with the board itself covered with black flannel material to which words, diagrams, lines, or other prepared items backed by a similar material will adhere when placed in position on the board. The conference leader must prepare his material in advance and practice the position and timing of how each item will be placed on the board.

In working with any of these visual aids, the leader should be careful to write or print clearly, arrange the items neatly, stand to the side to keep all the items in clear view, and not talk into the board rather than toward the group. A pointer should be used when necessary.

Handouts are materials prepared in advance in sufficient numbers to be passed out to each member, containing data, points to be taken up, cases, or other items. These are a helpful tool for stimulating interest and discussion. They should be comparatively brief, confined to one page on one side if possible. Their use should be carefully timed with the discussion to be held about them. Only the item being discussed should be in the group's hands at any one time. Care should be taken that members are not drawn into reading while they should be involved in pending discussion.

Demonstrations are used mostly in instructional situations where the leader or a member of the group shows the group how to do something or how a machine or other object operates. This usually involves *objects, models,* or other physical equipment. Some cautions are to be sure that the demonstration is in full view of the group, that it is not too long or cumbersome for the time available and the physical facilities, that it is properly integrated with the rest of the program or agenda, and that questions and points to be raised following the demonstration are worked out in advance.

Films, filmstrips, and *records* combine the visual with sound to make useful aids in many types of meetings. They are of most use in training conferences, or in public discussion programs, and some suggestions for using films as a basis for discussion are made in Chap. 11. These tools are rarely used in a staff conference. Some companies have put cases on records which dramatize the case as a method for bringing it before the group more realistically than by reading.

CASES AND SIMILAR DEVICES

The use of cases as a basis for bringing out points and principles by discussion has become well established, with the case method now one of the most commonly used methods for training, particularly in human relations principles. The case, which depicts a situation or problem among two or more individuals and what actually happened between them, is usually in printed narrative form and given to the members of a group for reading in advance of the conference. This is particularly true in the training conference. The individuals are asked to read it carefully and come prepared to discuss it at the next meeting. During the discussion, the leader draws out the facts of the problem and the solution as depicted in the case and then draws from the group the principles *they* feel the case shows in terms of what should have been done (the better solution), these then being the primary objectives of learning which the leader wanted the group to take from the meeting. There are many variants of this procedure, one being the more or less impromptu use of examples and incidents which the leader will bring up and state to the group orally during the meeting, and the group immediately starts its analysis. This shorter and simpler use of cases or examples can be employed profitably in any kind of conference in order to illustrate points under discussion.

The *incident process* [6] is one of several variants of the case method designed to bring group members into a closer feeling of involvement with the problem or situation and to stimulate more participation and discussion. This is in reality the case method, with the major variation of giving the group only a few facts about the incident to be discussed, thus requiring that the group draw the complete facts from the leader during the initial part of the discussion. During this period, no one expresses an opinion or point of view until all the facts are drawn out. Then the discussion proceeds as that of any case, usually with the goal of arriving at a specific solution. This method is said to get the group more closely involved, since the participants draw the facts from the leader rather than read the facts themselves; and the initial period fosters an attitude of *inquiry* and *investigation* which is not always present in the typical case method. It also makes unnecessary the reading of the case in advance of the meeting. These advantages may depend on how well either method is handled by the leader. The incident process requires more time in that the drawing-out period for the facts to be assembled must be considered, and there is the possibility that the leader may change the facts a little each time he gives them.

Role-playing (sometimes called "psychodrama" when used for

[6] See Paul and Faith Pigors, *The Incident Process: Case Studies in Management Development,* Bureau of National Affairs, Washington, D.C., 1955.

therapeutic purposes) is also a well-established method and achieves the greatest possible feeling of involvement by the participants to the situation under discussion. It is an actual dramatization of the case by members of the group, in front of others, after which the group discusses what they saw and how it might have been improved. Role-playing is most useful in dramatizing human relations situations, principles of interviewing and counseling, and all problems of interpersonal relations. The case or situation to be "acted out" is explained briefly by the leader. Then the members of the group are selected (or volunteer) to play the parts of the persons in the situation, which they proceed to do before the rest of the group. The leader then conducts discussion, raising questions and bringing out principles he has considered in advance. The degree of preparation for role-playing, as compared with doing it on the spur of the moment on a more or less impromptu basis, becomes a matter of question in using this tool. Some prefer that the dramatization be prepared in advance, others that it be done on the impromptu basis. It must be remembered that there are at least two major benefits of this method, the close feeling of involvement and understanding achieved by the total observing group and the even closer involvement felt by the actual participants in the dramatization. Probably more members can receive the latter benefit if it is employed more or less informally and oftener. If time permits and this is felt desirable, the situation can be acted out twice. Most role-playing incidents bring out the wrong way of doing things. After the discussion, during which correct principles are suggested, the right way can be acted out to show the group the way the incident should have been handled.

Still other variants of the case method are the recorded dramatization which we mentioned above and very brief incidents or "teasers," [7] which simply show the group a picture or drawing, such as a worker saying something to a supervisor with the supervisor's reply blank. The group is to fill in how he should reply.

[7] Prepared by Albert Mathews, "Ten Minute Training Tip," Hamilton Watch Company, Lancaster, Pa., 1954.

The case method and its variations involve careful planning and practice for expert leadership of its use, but the average conference leader can integrate the method in some way in searching for ways to stimulate discussion.

LISTENING

We include listening as a tool of leadership, just as we included it as a quality for the conference leader, for alert listening must be cultivated in order to achieve the maximum participation from a group. Although conference and group discussion should be across the table and between and among the members, we know how much the participant tends to speak toward the leader and to regard everything he says as reaching the leader's ears. Members will speak up much more actively and animatedly when they feel the leader is listening understandingly and sympathetically. As a leader, you must also follow closely all that is said in the discussion, so that you will know best how to conduct the meeting and what tools and methods to employ.

Leading Various Types of Conferences

It is rather dangerous to try to indicate just how one conference may differ from another in the leader's methods and tools or to imply that a certain type conference should always be conducted the same way and with the same methods. Throughout this chapter we have tried to point out the wide variety of principles that would affect this and the way the selection and use of various tools and methods would depend on many factors in the given situation. With these cautions in mind, then, we will show briefly what characteristics and tools of leadership tend to be applicable.

IN THE STAFF CONFERENCE

Being probably the most common type of conference, the staff conference brings forth the greatest variety of tools and methods.

The typical staff conference is a combination of items of information, explanation, or instruction to be given by the leader and problems to be solved or decisions reached. Leadership may go from a period of control by the leader to a period of group dominance of the outcome. Where he is presenting information, effective speaking, charts or a blackboard, and handouts might be useful. In solving problems, the leader must determine in advance the degree to which he will submit the final decision to the group. In stimulating discussion, he will plan the use of questions as his primary tool, along with brief analysis of cases or examples. He may use the case method or even role-playing more fully in a longer conference or where the problem at hand needs more careful analysis. He will arrange for a secretary to keep minutes and prepare a report and possibly for an observer to analyze the conference.

IN THE COMMITTEE

The committee is usually a problem-solving group which deliberates very informally and has as its objective the preparation of its specific recommendations as a report. The emphasis on leadership is extreme informality. The period of fact-finding and inquiry should be thorough and detailed. Research tends to show that the ideal size for committee deliberation is about seven members, who should be seated face to face so that maximum interpersonal speaking is achieved. The leader's agenda in a committee is not nearly as rigid as in the average staff conference. Usually more time is allowed, for a committee can make its own decisions as to length of meetings and frequency. The leader is also inclined to allow an exchange between two members to continue at greater length in committee. His primary tools are questions, transitions and summaries, handouts, and recording of progress on blackboard or charts. Since the report is the final objective, the chairman will see that machinery is established for writing this. Committees are inclined to make more use of voting and parliamentary procedure than a conference, so that parliamentary procedure will have to be understood by the group.

IN THE TRAINING OR INSTRUCTIONAL CONFERENCE

We have pointed out that many conferences, and particularly the staff conference, include objectives which are to inform or instruct. Depending on the extent and importance of this, the leader would employ tools and methods more typically useful in the training conference. We indicated in Chap. 7 that the training conference is a somewhat specialized use of the conference method, and expert leadership is developed by training and personnel directors, training instructors, and other staff officials, and sometimes by operating management supervisors who are called on to instruct in a major company program. When such is the case, they are (or should be) brought together in a series of meetings in which their ability to teach by the conference method is developed. In all learning situations, we are striving more and more for greater group participation to achieve better learning. In the school systems and the college classroom alike, the discussion method led by the instructor and the use of panels and other programs to stimulate discussion of the subject-matter principles being learned are more common all the time. Our discussion of some of these methods in Chap. 11, including the film-forum, are in point here.

Particularly in dealing with adults who have had some actual experience with the application of the principles to be learned in a training situation, we have found that they will accept, understand, and better apply the principles if they have a part in shaping them during a conference discussion. This is perhaps the essential value of the conference medium for training purposes. The tools for the leader are the use of questions, considerable emphasis on the developmental charts and blackboard material during the discussion, occasionally the prepared chart and the flannel board, and strong emphasis on handouts. The case method, including role-playing, incidents, and recordings, is also relied on strongly to bring out instructional principles by the conference method.

Our earlier discussion in this chapter indicated that the training and instructional conference is more strongly controlled by the leader than the problem-solving conference. This is true largely because he is responsible for seeing that the proper principles to be learned are brought out during the discussion. He should do this through the adroit use of questions rather than direct statement or experting on his part, although some direct teaching is frequently necessary.

IN THE LARGE MEETING OR CONFERENCE

How large a conference should get is a matter of degree, and we have pointed out that the ideal size is about ten to fifteen members. When the group gets quite large, as in an assembly of all the members at a convention or the listening audience at a lecture or speech, it is difficult to achieve very much group participation. The tools to be used are a forum period during which individual members ask questions or make comments to be answered by the speaker, dividing the assembly into smaller discussion groups to discuss the speaker's topic, as we discuss under the buzz-session technique in Chap. 11, and audience panels. The latter method calls up several members of the audience to the front to sit in a panel or colloquy arrangement with the speaker and the chairman to discuss the topic and raise questions. Another tool is the workshop method of dividing the entire assembly into smaller groups, each of which adjourns to a separate room to discuss further the speaker's topic under the guidance of a leader. The assembly may or may not come back together with individual questions or comments from each group, as in the buzz-session technique. Sometimes the entire group can be seated at separate tables initially, as at a dinner. They listen to a speaker, followed by a period of discussion among themselves. Or there may be no speaker, and each table group proceeds to discuss a topic or problem for the purpose of arriving at conclusions, questions, or proposals. Then they may choose a leader to present these to the total group.

IN THE INTERVIEW

In our earlier classification of types of private discussion situations, we included the interview as a two-person conference. We do not usually regard the person calling or conducting the interview as a "leader," but rather we think of the interview as involving close interpersonal communication between two people. Most of the principles in Chap. 7 on interpersonal relations would apply, and we point out their application to the interview more fully in that chapter.

On Recognizing Participants

As a leader of discussion, you will always have the problem of what method you use for recognizing individual participants and "giving them the floor" when they indicate a desire to speak. A strong word of caution is given here to establish as informal and spontaneous a method as possible, commensurate with the type of meeting and the degree of informality that can be achieved. Surely in the average small conference group, members should be encouraged to speak up when they want to and not seek your permission by raising a hand or otherwise asking you if they may speak. Each individual, of course, has the responsibility to do this tactfully and without interrupting a speaker, as we point out in Chap. 7. Most of our suggestions for both the leader and participants in the panel, in Chap. 11, would also apply here.

You as a leader will set the climate and pattern to be followed, and your manner as well as your comments to the group will indicate to what extent they should feel free to speak up. Sometimes when several people want to speak, some way of indicating this to you as a leader is necessary. But an expression on the face, leaning forward, maybe a movement of the hand will all reveal this desire so as to make the actual raising of the hand unnecessary. An otherwise informal conversational atmosphere which a good conference wants to achieve is made stilted and cumbersome with hands waving around the group. In a larger, more formal, or business meeting under parliamentary procedure, or in a forum period, such method of recognition, or even standing, may be desirable.

The nature of the meeting, how well you know each other, and the degree of informality will determine whether you and other members call each other by first names.

Conclusion

In this chapter we have tried to explore and explain leadership as an attitude and a philosophy which may be even a way of life, as possessing certain essential qualities, as embracing many responsibilities, and as including a number of specific tools and methods. We have emphasized the extreme importance of the leader to the successful conference or discussion situation while we have also analyzed his role as changing from a strong to weak position in relation to the group and the objective to be accomplished. We have presented different points of view and theories on leadership style and methods. Then we have seen some of the specific applications of leadership tools and methods in different kinds of meetings.

This all adds up to a very important and complex part of the entire process of achieving ability and skill in conference and discussion. Essentially leadership is not a bag of tricks, mechanical rules, or panacea formulas and methods that will automatically insure success in a given case. It does require a knowledge of the tools and methods and accepted principles developed as we learn more and more about group behavior. Then it requires resourcefulness, initiative, imagination, and adaptation of your best abilities and skills that can be brought to bear in each successive challenge you face as a leader.

APPLYING THIS CHAPTER

1. What do you feel is the relative importance of leadership and participation in discussion? Has the reading of this chapter influenced your conclusions?
2. Compare various types of leaders in conferences you have attended.
3. Make a complete evaluation of a leader in a conference you have attended recently.
4. What major problems of leadership have you encountered or observed in other leaders? What would you now do to resolve these?
5. Note the leader's use of questions in a conference. To what extent were they overhead or general? Direct? Did he make any mistakes in using direct questions inappropriately? What can you suggest to him in his future use of questions in conference leading?
6. Have you observed a member trying to assume the leader's role and responsibilities? Was it because of the leader's inadequacy or because of the member's aggressiveness? How was this received by the group?
7. What is the relative importance of the leader's attitude and his expertness in using tools and techniques in running a good conference?
8. In anticipating your next conference, plan your use of the blackboard or chart easel, working out your headings carefully in advance. Similarly, plan the use of a handout, a case, and role-playing if this will help the group better see a problem.

CHAPTER 7

Participation

UNFORTUNATELY, less attention is paid to participation in conference and discussion than to leadership, yet the average person has many more experiences and responsibilities in the participant's role. All too frequently, we enter a conference room and sit down at the table as group members with scarcely more thought about our place in the meeting than to be in the proper room at the proper time. Our tendency to ignore preparation for our role as participants grows out of at least two misconceptions: the thought that the only really important person at a conference is the leader, who therefore has the total responsibility for its success, and the conclusion that the participant's role is of little significance. In addition, we expand the second misconception to believe that there is so little to the role that of course we can do all that is required as participants, or we believe that nothing much can be done to develop our ability in this direction anyway.

Fortunately, we know that none of these conclusions are sound and that much effort is being expended in recent years to discover just what the role of an individual group member is, how it relates to others in the group and to the leader, and how individuals can work best together to achieve a cooperative group objective. And we also know that we are paying more attention to principles, methods, and tools which the average person can study and master and make of himself a better group member. Our objective in this chapter is to analyze the participant's role in relation to others, to indicate his responsibilities, and to make some suggestions.

The Dynamics of Participation

Every participant in a small group discussion such as a conference is in direct and dynamic relationship with everyone else in the room. He communicates unilaterally with each person in the group and with the leader, yet every participant is a listener and reacts in some way to every communication which appears to be between just two persons. A very complex and changing relationship thus develops and expands in every direction in a network of exchanges. The communicative processes of speaking and listening, always with the role of speaker or listener changing from one participant to another, soon draws each member of the group into a stronger and stronger feeling of involvement with the total dynamics of the group process as a whole. *Discussion dynamics,* then, as we pointed out in Chap. 2, concerns these relationships within the group and the total group involvement that each person feels as he is drawn more closely into the group.

The participant in a small group that has been stimulated toward an active, animated, and sensitive exchange of thought and feeling on a problem probably feels a stronger degree of involvement than he does in any other type of communicative situation. If we compare the sending and receiving process in communicating through writing and reading with that of speaking and listening in ordinary situations and with that of participating in a small group or in interpersonal relations of emotional involvement, we would find a progression of feeling mounting toward the latter situation in most cases. In other words, communicating through writing or reading usually finds the communicator by himself and in a detached mood. In making a speech or speaking in the usual conversational situations, or in listening in either of these, the individual communicator is with others, senses their reactions and their presence, and probably feels more involved than when writing or reading. There may be such situations where he feels very much involved if the subject is close to his emotional interests or if the other communicator stirs such emotional feelings. In the group situation, however, there is a combination of interpersonal relations and the effect of these on the group as a whole which develops the close feeling of involvement that usually is not felt in other situations. This would of course not always be the case, and any of the other communicative mediums and settings might arouse the greatest possible involvement in the individual participants under certain circumstances. The general tendency for increased feeling of involvement in the group or in closely related interpersonal communication is shown in Fig. 7-1. The figures and the relationship of the three situations are only suggested.

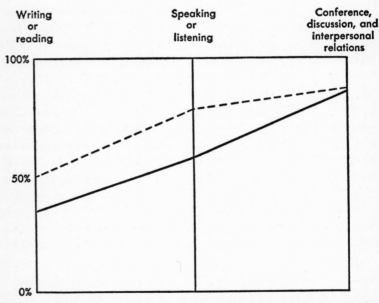

Fig. 7-1 Relationship of feeling of involvement by the individual in different communicative situations.

We are learning some interesting things about *quantity* and *quality* of participation both as to how these affect the relationships among the members and the effectiveness of the contributions given. The Conference Research Project at the University of Michigan and the Laboratory of Social Relations at Harvard University came to similar conclusions with regard to high quantity of participation.[1] The individuals who talk the most in a conference usually contribute the highest quality of remarks as well and tend to have the best ideas. They also tend to contribute more problem-solving remarks constructively rather than time-wasting or negative remarks. There is also a tendency for the persons making the most remarks to be on the receiving end of questions and remarks directed at them by others to a greater extent than silent members. The frequent participant is thus respected by the group for his comments, unless, of course, they are obviously meaningless and just the result of a desire to be heard. Actually, the most talkative member is probably not the best-liked member in the group, yet he is likely to rate high in this respect. We can conclude that we should not automatically condemn the high-quantity talker in a group.

In Chap. 6, we commented on the many reasons that an individual may remain silent in a group and that it is well for the leader to keep these in mind. From the standpoint of the participant, he should try to break away from his self-centered thoughts and project himself into the mood, feelings, and issues that are before the group. The earlier he does this in a conference, the more effective his total contributions will be. The participant who enters the discussion early or at the very outset of the meeting tends to establish a reputation among the group members. Once he has gained such a reputation for expressing himself well, his

[1] Jack N. Peterman, "Verbal Participation—Its Relation to Decision Satisfaction and the Leader Function in Decision-making Groups," Conference Research Project, Ann Arbor, Mich., 1948 (mimeographed release), and Robert F. Bales, "How People Interact in Conferences," *Scientific American,* vol. 192, March, 1955.

later comments will be looked upon more favorably and he will be respected for his judgment and opinion. His *status* in the group is thus strengthened through this type of *personal proof* which he has advanced of his own ability and value to the group.

Participation may be offered in so many forms that many attempts have been made to classify the types of contributions members of a group may make. No such classification is completely satisfactory, and lists which attempt to include all types of remarks can get quite cumbersome and long. The most constructive classification is in terms of the contribution in relation to the total group objective. The two research groups mentioned above developed these lists of types of remarks made by conference participants:

LIST A	LIST B
Shows solidarity	Goal-setting
Shows tension release	Problem-proposing
Shows agreement	Information-seeking
Gives suggestion	Information-giving
Gives opinion	Solution-proposing
Gives information	Development-seeking
Asks for information	Opposing
Asks for opinion	Supporting
Asks for suggestions	Summary-seeking
Shows disagreement	Summary-giving
Shows tension	Non-problem-directed
Shows antagonism	

These boil down to four or five major purposes of speaking up in a discussion:

• To offer or seek information, or to clarify.

• To offer or seek opinion. This could be for or against the proposal under consideration or the goal of the conference. It could also result from or induce argument and tension.

• To offer or to seek solutions.

• To summarize, make transitions, or otherwise help "lead" the conference.

It would be unrealistic and even undesirable to expect an equal distribution of participation as to quantity among all members and as to kind of contribution among the various types listed above. This would assume that every individual could be cast into the role of the "typical" participant and that all would fit into the same mold. Observation does indicate that there tends to be an approximate balance in most meetings between questions, answers, and reactions among the remarks made. In the democratic discussion process, we do not want all remarks to be positive, for we know the value of negative and questioning remarks of the opposition in shaping the best conclusions and decisions. The important thing, from the standpoint of positive and negative remarks, is to avoid too intense a conflict and too much tension when argument develops. The democratic process also gives everyone an equal right to be heard and therefore makes available to him as much quantity of participation as any other participant, yet we would not want or expect that all members speak an equal amount. If this were sought as a goal by a leader or the participants, the result would probably be a stilted, mechanical process with everyone bent on counting his and others' contributions rather than on following the discussion itself.

Interpersonal Relations

Participation in discussion is largely a series of interpersonal relationships between you and others in the room, including primarily the other participants, the leader, and the group as a whole. In the strict sense, the leader is not included, for he should not be a participant. Yet every member of the group has a constant relationship with the leader which has some influence on his relations with others. Except for the fact that it is multiplied and made more complex because of all the cross currents and the pyramiding of feelings and reactions that can develop in a group, the close interpersonal relations of any one member with another differs little from your day-to-day contacts with people. One who has developed an understanding and a liking for people, who has a friendly and sympathetic attitude in his general dealings with others, and who therefore respects the thoughts and feelings of others as part of his daily living habits will find that all these attributes are applicable in the conference.

Interpersonal relations, then, include no new considerations or magic formulas in discussion situations except the awareness of the fact that they exist in a total group environment which produces the discussion dynamics and the feeling of involvement on which we have just commented.

Interpersonal communication is the fundamental basis of our interpersonal relations and likewise of the whole discussion process. The network of a discussion pattern that develops in a conference comes from a series of exchanges among the members, which involve one person talking and another listening. It will be well for us to lift this communicative relationship between two people out of the conference room and analyze it so that we understand it better. To begin with, it is an exceedingly complex process even though it involves only two people. This is as much because each person is indeed complex in himself as it is because of the difficulties encountered when one tries to make the other understand. Rarely do the communicator and the listener come from such similar backgrounds of experience, interests, feelings, prejudices, and positions that they think exactly alike or use the same language. All of these may create barriers to successful communication.

There are some characteristics of the communication process which must be understood. *First,* it is a two-way process, not a one-way street from speaker to listener. As the speaker talks, the listener reacts and thus influences the speaker. Thoughts and reactions are exchanged between the two as the process really becomes more than two-way and develops into a *circular process,* as shown in the diagram. *Second,* at least as much consideration must be given to the *skill of listening* as to the skill of speaking. Listening is an active part of communication. *Third,* all communication takes place in some particular *situation,* not in a vacuum. In a conference, the situation is the conference room and the other members of the group; in a conversation it is the specific setting and environment. Both speaker and listener must relate what they say and hear to the situation at hand. *Fourth,* there are always *barriers* that are constantly thwarting the process of communication. The way in which these relate to each other is shown in Fig. 7-2.

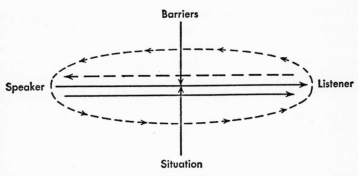

Fig. 7-2 Interpersonal communication as a circular process, showing the relationship of barriers and the situation.

Showing the effect of barriers on the communication process in another way, we can list those that appear to cause the most trouble in the center of an arrow from speaker to listener and then attempt to show on either side the things that both speaker and listener must do to break through the barriers. We should be wary that this may appear to oversimplify the problem.

Resolving most of the barriers to communication is a matter of speaking and listening as much as possible with the other person's position and interests in mind. This emphasizes the importance of our suggestions for individual and group analysis in earlier

BARRIERS TO COMMUNICATION

SPEAKER should:		LISTENER should:
1. Speak at level of listeners' status, interests, experiences	1. Different status, position, self-experiences	1. Think in terms of speaker's status, interests, experiences
2. Adapt to listener prejudices	2. Prejudices	2. Dispel prejudices
3. Use common ground and "you" attitude	3. "I" versus "you" attitude	3. Develop "you" attitude
4. Make changes seem attractive	4. Resistance to change	4. Be open-minded
5. Organize clearly for understanding	5. Refute rather than understand	5. Listen to understand, not to refute
6. Develop ideas for listener interest	6. Extra time to listen	6. Use listening time constructively
7. Use listener level language	7. Language	7. Analyze speaker's language

chapters and the need for the participant to think in terms of other members of a group both as he speaks and as he listens. We are all full of prejudices and self-interests, and we tend to like what we have approved of up to now. That is why most people resist changes and therefore try to find reasons against a proposal as listeners. And if speakers would be more successful, they should suggest changes while pointing out their advantages to the listener and that they are not much different from the *status quo* after all. The language of the speaker should be selected with the listener in mind, but if it is not, the listener should strive to understand the meaning the *speaker* intended from the words as *he* spoke them.

Listening is regarded by most people as a passive part of communication in which one would receive just that part of a message that happened to penetrate or seem attractive. We do know that the rate of ability to comprehend what we hear is three or four times faster than the average person speaks, which is about 125 words per minute. In other words, listeners have "extra" time which they should use constructively to analyze the speaker, reconstruct his purpose and his main ideas, apply what he is saying, and evaluate. Instead we tend to daydream and let our minds wander away from the speaker while we smugly feel that we are either way ahead of him in our thinking or that we don't regard what he's saying as important anyway. Listening must be an active and constructive process. It is discussed more fully later in this chapter as a participant's responsibility.

In the *conference,* in *informal conversation,* and in *our daily contacts* with others, interpersonal communication is spontaneous, lively, animated, and even unpredictable. Participation in all such situations should be alert and always adapted to what is taking place in the group and to the interests of group members.

In the *interview,* participation is generally more planned and structured. It usually follows a pattern or sequence worked out in advance by the person who called the interview. Both persons are more on guard and more formal, and both should have studied carefully the other person involved, the subject or nature of the interview, and the situation in which it takes place. In Chap. 4 we discussed the interview as a two-person conference, with the objective being to solve a problem (or to sell or persuade the other person to accept a proposal, product, or idea, as in the sales interview or the persuasive situation where you are trying to get your superior to adopt a suggestion) or to seek information (where one person draws information and facts from the other). Other types of interview objectives are to handle a grievance or reprimand with an employee and the job application.

The person seeking the interview (interviewer) should decide on his objective and the probable pattern the discussion will take, that is, a problem-solution-action pattern or an informational–drawing-out pattern as discussed in earlier chapters. He should then make a careful analysis of the other person (interviewee). He should prepare the *approach* and greeting; the *opening remarks* or questions to be raised; the degree of emphasis on the *need* or *problem* phase of the discussion; the point at which the *solution* (plan, proposal, product) will be introduced in relation to the need or problem or whether both phases will be developed together; the way in which he will advance *points* and *supporting proof* of his proposal; the way in which *questions* and *objections* raised by the other person will be met; and the timing and manner of effecting the *close* in terms of the action to be taken, or the decision to be reached. This is the logical sequence for most interviews.

In the job application interview, the applicant is usually on the persuading end and must put his best foot forward in showing how he is the best solution to the need or problem (job to be filled). He must also be alert in answering questions raised by the person representing the company and seeking the proper individual to fill the job.

The interpersonal relations and the communication between individuals in an interview is very much the same as in any exchange between two persons in a discussion, within the framework of the more structured pattern for their exchange and the specific objective each participant has anticipated in advance. Although we speak of the interview as more structured than most informal discussion, this is not always the case. In many interview situations, particularly in counseling and the handling of human relations problems, the person conducting the interview should do all he can to create a permissive and free atmosphere in which the other person will feel that he wants to and can reveal his thoughts and feelings fully without being guided or directed. This so-called *nondirective* method of interviewing puts the interviewer in the role of remaining silent as much as he can, avoiding leading the other person, making little if any comment except to have him go on talking, and never revealing a point of view, agreement, or disagreement. The fundamental principle here is to let the other person work out the solution to his own problem by talking it out fully and gradually realizing what can be done.

Human relations and the general endeavor to improve the way each of us gets along with others is the broad goal of all interpersonal communication, and it is part of the goal in any discussion. We cannot avoid the consideration of others around the table as *people* and not as inanimate objects. That is why no one who would get along with others and be successful in his relations with them can fail to consider their feelings and interests. It is why one must listen for understanding while trying to locate *areas of agreement* or *common ground,* rather than ways to refute. It is why one should not stick dogmatically to an opposing position when a proper attitude of inquiry and open-mindedness would show the other person to be right.

This does not mean that you should never feel free to oppose a point, to refute it with all the sincerity and evidence you can muster, and to advance your own position forcefully and effectively. Everyone has this right, and he would not be honest with himself or with the group if he did not forthrightly express his opinion. But from the standpoint of human relations and group cooperation, one must be careful of the *manner* in which he does this. The biggest difficulty in attaining cooperative discussion is when disagreement creates tension and bitterness between the participants. The important thing, then, is to use *tact* and an attitude of *conciliation* in answering the point or argument of another person.

Conciliation can be practiced without weakening your own position. It is largely a matter of your initial handling of the point made by the other person (we never like to speak of him as an "opponent" in discussion). If you start out by calling him "foolish," "ignorant," or "utterly lacking in common sense," you are using language that is insulting and that is bound to induce an equally strong reply from him. In the second place, you are attacking the man rather than his point, which is one of the best ways to destroy human relations. There is usually some good basis for the point in *his* mind, just as you feel that your own points are good. As you take up his point, do it in a pleasant manner and try to avoid such words as "disagree" in stating your own position. Here are some specific suggestions for conciliatory refutation. There are other suggestions for refutation in relation to debate in Chap. 11.

1. Listen and understand his point clearly, evaluating it and not the man who is speaking. But try to analyze why *he* is making this point.
2. Determine to what extent you can accept the point before you quickly assume that it has no value at all. Look for areas of agreement.
3. State his point accurately when you start to answer it, then state your position in relation to it.
4. Support and prove your position with reasoning and evidence.
5. Speak convincingly and enthusiastically, yet without showing anger or in too dogmatic a manner.
6. Be sure your position is clear when you finish. Restate and summarize for clarity.

The Participant's Responsibilities

Much of what we have said thus far adds up to the responsibilities of the participant as a member of a discussion group. We have already made clear that he has a responsibility to prepare for the meeting and to recognize that its success results from capable and cooperative participation even more than from good leadership. Some principles and methods for participation have also been discussed. Let's bring together the responsibilities under four major headings.

PARTICIPANT'S RESPONSIBILITIES

Develop a proper attitude
Have respect for other members
Help shape goals and decisions
Participate appropriately

• A *proper attitude* is one of cooperation toward the group and the objective of the meeting and one of inquiry and open-mindedness toward the discovery of the best decisions for the good of the most people. To expect this fully might be unrealistic, at least in some group situations, and it might be the same sort of a quest that we make for the "ideal" conference leader. Actually, it is quite understandable that you will go into a conference after considerable studying of the agenda and with a deep conviction for some particular plan or point of view that you think should be incorporated in the decision. You may also plan ways and means to get support for your plan from other members of the group who are known to be sympathetic; and you may plan the way in which you will present your points, the proof to be used, and the timing of your remarks, all to gain this end. This is not entirely wrong, as we pointed out above in regard to your right to advance your position with conviction when refuting another person's remarks. As a matter of fact, this is the way democracy works, and it is incumbent on you to do the best job you can of presenting your points.

There is a happy balance, however, between meek submission to anything that is suggested just to insure good human relations and the other extreme of strong, dogmatic, stubborn insistence that everyone else is wrong and you are right. It is this balance that we strive for and that brings a healthy give-and-take among the participants. Though you have prepared well and advanced good proof of your position, you should still listen and consider objectively the points and proof presented for other proposals, or against yours, and be willing to conciliate and cooperate toward the best conclusion. It is this kind of attitude that we are suggesting.

• A *respect for other members* and for what they say has already been stressed in regard to the need for understanding their background, position, interests, feelings, and prejudices in regard to answering their points in a pleasant and conciliatory manner. After you have developed a proper attitude in this regard, probably the most important aspect of your responsibility to respect others is the *way you listen* to them. Listening becomes a major tool as well as a responsibility for the participant in a conference. We have said that all listening must be active and alert, not simply a passive process. This is of greatest importance in the group situation, where you have to listen to a number of people rather than just one. And unfortunately there is a tendency in a group to listen only to those whom you like or whose point of view will coincide with yours.

It requires a great deal of alertness to follow all that is said in a conference. As one member is talking, his point seems of little or no relevance at the time, yet it may turn out later to be a vital point which you should have remembered. Listening must be very alert because of the need to retain what is being said and to relate it to future remarks as the conference progresses. If you listen well and retain a point until later, you may find you can much better reply to it than try to refute it hastily. You may find it very worthwhile to take notes as others speak, jotting down essential facts and information and opinions that are expressed by individuals. You may later want to comment on several of these and refer to persons by name. You will want to take mental note at least of the way other members seem to be reacting, in which direction sentiment seems to be swinging, what individuals are for or against different proposals. All of this demands alert and active listening.

Your *physical listening manner* should be animated and expressive. There is such a thing as an animated listener, just as there is this quality in effective speaking. This should show in your face, in your eyes, and in your physical bearing. You know how much you respect the person who looks directly at you, eyes open, letting you know he is eager to hear you. Just remember this when you establish your own listening habits at a meeting. Slouching in a chair, leaning on elbows, chin on hand, or playing with a pencil are not the characteristics of a good listener.

You have a further responsibility in this respect at a meeting, for your actions as a listener are contagious in relation to others.

It will soon become evident that you are bored or indifferent to what is being said, and this breeds either ill feeling or a tendency to join you in your indifference.

Summarizing our suggestions for good listening in conference, let's try to:

1. Listen alertly, in both attitude and physical bearing.
2. Listen to everyone with equal interest.
3. Analyze the point being made with respect to whether it furthers the group interest, your own interest, or the self-interest of the speaker.
4. Analyze the relationship of the remark to the total discussion.
5. Take notes (but don't let this interfere with your participation).
6. Keep shifting and weaving the remarks together and relating them to the group goal.

• In *helping to shape goals and decisions,* you assume your responsibility along with other members and the leader for the successful outcome of the meeting. This responsibility adds up to doing just about everything we are suggesting in this chapter. It does not mean, however, that you should not feel free to sponsor or join a minority that is opposed to the majority of the members. Again, this is a healthy characteristic of democracy, and minorities are helpful for refining and improving on majority decisions and bringing about progress in our thinking. We comment more fully on the total process of decision-making in Chap. 8, including this relationship. In our earlier discussion of conference planning, we pointed out that every member also has a responsibility to help the leader keep the discussion organized. We might list these specific ways in which a member should help shape and guide the discussion toward the desired outcome:

1. Keep within the approximate agenda as indicated by the leader. In so doing, avoid bringing up hidden agendas that are irrelevant to the purpose of the meeting.
2. Avoid lengthy speeches and arguments that are time-consuming and not productive toward the purpose.
3. Make or suggest making internal summaries or transitions if the

leader is not doing these well, in order to keep the organization of the discussion clearly before the group.

4. Think constructively toward supporting proposals that seem to be in the best interest of the group, consistent with your own opinions and judgment. Make supporting and affirmative remarks when you can do so honestly and avoid unnecessary negative remarks.

• *Appropriate participation* is your end goal as a group member and is what this entire chapter deals with. In the purely physical sense of what you do and say as a participant, we could make a few specific suggestions (as we do below) on your speaking in conference and limit this chapter to these suggestions. But we have wanted to emphasize that what you actually say and do is the result and outcome of the many considerations and principles we have discussed up to now. Your speech is not something just tacked on externally through the symbols of voice, actions, and language. It is the outward expression of your feelings, interests, opinions, relationships, and background as you show these through the use of the principles and tools you use to make yourself an effective person. That is a chief reason why we put actual participation last on our list of responsibilities. *You must have a proper attitude, a respect for others, a desire and ability to listen, and a willingness to help shape group goals if you are to participate well as a speaker in group discussion.*

We have already made some suggestions bearing on individual participation from the standpoint of timing, frequency, and relations with others. Let's tie these together with these principles:

1. Participate early so that you make your presence known and felt throughout the meeting.
2. Feel free to participate often as long as you have something to say. High participation is not necessarily disliked by other group members.
3. Supply information and facts when you can and when they will be useful to the group. Ask questions seeking information as appropriate.

4. Vary your participation from questions, information, opinion, and proof.
5. Time your participation appropriately. Do not make lengthy remarks at any one time; one minute is ordinarily enough. Do not make a series of points at one time. It is better to contribute several different times, making just one point at a time.
6. In answering a point of another member, after you have done this, use the opportunity to make a transition and introduce a new point, if you deem this to be an appropriate and opportune time for the new point.
7. Avoid argument and taking issue with others during the early part of a problem-solving discussion, when the problem is being analyzed and when solutions are first being offered.
8. In taking issue with another, use the principles of tact and conciliation.
9. In advancing a point, use sound reasoning and good evidence and proof. Have a good supply of factual evidence on hand, so that you can keep adding it to your remarks, rather than going over old evidence too much.
10. Use language that others understand. Stop and define or explain new terms. Always make your purpose and your meaning clear.
11. When contributing a point of view or more facts on a point that had been under discussion earlier in the conference, be sure that the group understands clearly what point you are now dealing with.
12. When appropriate, use persuasive methods to win others over to your points. Appeal to basic emotional drives, common interests and experiences, and the senses.
13. Use the pronouns "we" and "you" more frequently than "I" in order to indicate group interests.
14. Contribute spontaneously without being called on, as long as you don't interrupt a speaker. But be ready to come in with your point as soon as he is finished, or someone else might beat you to it.

As for your *manner of speaking*, the good conference participant remembers that every remark he makes should be spoken effectively and with consideration for the basic principles of good speech. We are quite apt to forget these in the conference, since it is an informal situation and induces us to lapse into habits of expression that are ineffective. Conference speaking should be conversational, not generally loud or forceful. Yet it must be animated and enthusiastic. Sloppy posture, indirectness, mumbling, and other similar tendencies should be avoided. Here are some characteristics your remarks should have:

1. A lively sense of communication as a whole, in which you indicate that you are speaking to the group, both in the degree of physical animation you show and the degree of voice projection necessary for the situation.
2. A direct communicative manner toward the particular person for whom your remarks are intended, if such is the case.
3. Clear and distinct enunciation of your words so that they can be heard by everyone and clearly understood.
4. Use of gesture and expression of you as a total person, through facial expression, the hands, or other indication of physical animation.
5. A proper degree of emphasis and force, with appropriate variety and modulation.

Conclusion

Do not take lightly your responsibility as a participant in a discussion group. Prepare for it, plan for it, and develop a proper attitude for it. Remember that the small group situation probably brings you into a closer feeling of involvement in relation to others than most of your communicative situations. Group discussion is dynamic and animated, and it involves your relations with other people and with the group as a whole, with the subject, the goals, and the issues that may come up influencing your total involvement. Good participation is primarily a matter of interpersonal relations and communication with people. You must develop a cooperative and understanding attitude in relation to other participants, respect what they say, listen to them, avoid dogmatic argument, and help bring about the group goals. Yet you should do all you can to further your own honest interests and convictions through the most effective speaking you can do as a participant, while you are also doing all you can as a good listener.

APPLYING THIS CHAPTER

1. Make a list of the types of participants you have observed in various discussion situations. Analyze why they participated as they did in each case.
2. Practice using the steps of conciliation the next time you get into an argument or, better still, don't let the argument develop.
3. Each of four participants made this statement in reply to a point made in a conference. Analyze each:
   a. "That's nonsense! I don't believe a word of it. Why don't you read the newspapers?"
   b. "Your point is an interesting one, and from where you sit it may be logical. But I wonder whether some additional facts might lead to the same conclusion. . ."
   c. "The point you make might seem good to you, but I disagree! I think. . ."
   d. "That's a good point. I'd like to support it. . ."
4. Make a list of disagreements between you and others at a conference, and try to analyze why these arose.
5. Note the most talkative and the most quiet members in your next conference. Look behind their participation and determine what caused this kind of participation.
6. Make a complete analysis of someone you plan to interview. Can you think of an interview where one factor handled differently might have influenced its outcome if you had known something about this prior to the interview?

CHAPTER 8

Decision-making and Evaluation

SOMETIMES THE OBJECTIVES of a conference are measured according to the decisions made and the action taken. We also know that many conferences and other discussion meetings never reach decisions and actually did not have this as an original objective. Whether the purpose is to arrive at very specific decisions and courses of action, to pass on information, or simply to talk things over, we do want to know how well we succeeded and whether, in retrospect, we had a successful conference. We are therefore taking up in this chapter the process of decision-making and of evaluation, since both are concerned with results.

The major types of meetings concerned with reaching decisions are the problem-solving and policy-making conference and the business meeting of the average organization, which is usually conducted under parliamentary procedure. Most public discussion programs have as their objectives the stimulating of thought and the opportunity for the members of a group to air points of view. As we point out in later chapters, it is rare that a panel or symposium discussion before a larger group would reach a decision as to the subject or problem under discussion.

The decision-making process is part of the final stage of discussion wherein the group determines (if it has been given this responsibility by the leader and by the nature of the problem before it) the desired outcome and the action to be taken. The decision thus follows the problem analysis, the suggested solutions, and the critical examination of possible solutions. As the group converges toward the best solution it must then make decisions. The decision-making process is thus regarded as part of the final solution and of the action steps in the total conference process.

Basic Considerations in Decision-making

There is no formal procedure for arriving at decisions in conferences. Actually the preference is to avoid procedure completely and to try to arrive at group feeling and judgment in other ways, particularly in situations where as much permissiveness as possible is given to the group. Where informal methods are desired, a number of questions can be raised to shed some light on the process of decision-making, how decisions are reached, and their value.

• *Whose decision is it?* This is a rather basic question and strikes at the heart of the management of the conference in terms of the relationship between leader and group control. If circumstances, or the type of leadership, are such that the leader is going to make the decisions, he should tell the group this and indicate to them the extent to which he will rely on their judgment. In an informational or instructional conference, the conclusions are probably going to be more the leader's than the group's. It is the problem-solving conference that requires not only a clear understanding between the leader and the group as to who will make the decision but also agreement on the method to be used in reaching it, if this can be done. Ideally the group should make the decisions where the leader has indicated he wants their combined judgment in solving a problem. Yet even this kind of conference subject may not permit complete freedom of decision by the group if the leader knows the policies and frame of reference within which he must report the outcome and therefore knows that the group's decision must fit into organizational policy already established. His honesty and sincerity in explaining just how much the group is free to make its own decision will help considerably.

Executives and supervisors are not consistent in the practice of letting the group make the decision during a conference even in problem-solving situations where they seek the group's advice. Asked how they used the conference in helping them make decisions on problems for which they had responsibility, some 65 per cent said that decisions were actually made at the conference, based on the discussion of the group and the combined judgment of the members. The other 35 per cent said they used the conference only as preliminary to their final decision, or as *advisory* in helping them make the decision after the conference was over. Many executives indicate that such a decision might be made while seated at their own desks reflecting on what happened in the conference.[1]

Another aspect of the question "Whose decision is it?" is the actual phrasing of the decision by the leader in relation to the group's approval. The question here is the nature of the leader's closing remarks, in which he states what he thinks the decision to be. More than 60 per cent of executives polled said they phrased the decision in their own words and then asked the group generally whether or not this was properly stated and whether anyone took exception or wished to suggest a different wording. Another 12 per cent said they stated the decision in their own words and then went around the table asking each member directly whether he approved the wording or wished to restate it. Some 16 per cent said they stated the decision in their own words and assumed that this would be the final wording and would be acceptable to the group, without any check with the group or to specific members. As a general rule, the leader should best summarize and state what he thinks the group's thinking is as accurately as possible

[1] Martin Kriesberg, "Executives Evaluate Administrative Conferences," *Advanced Management,* vol. 15, March, 1950.

and then ask them if his statement reflects their combined conclusions. We go into this more fully under consensus below.

Finally, in answering the question of whether it is the group's or the leader's decision, we should remember that the ideal goal of problem-solving meetings is to leave the outcome and the decision in the hands of the group as much as possible. When this cannot be done, the leader should be clear and frank as to who will make the decision and as to why it is made this way.

• *How good a decision is it?* The question of the value and quality of a group's decision as compared with the decision of one person is one that has been pondered by students of the conference method at least since the days of Socrates. Modern writers and researchers generalize more and more in favor of the group decision. There is no conclusive evidence to prove that a group can make *better* decisions than an individual in a given case, for there are many variables that affect such judgment and it is difficult to generalize. We do know that modern management has fully accepted the concept that members of a work group should be called on for advice and judgment as much as possible in solving problems and in making decisions that concern their own work. We know that participation in a decision is a key factor in having the individual group member feel that it is a good decision and one that he wants to carry out. There is considerable evidence to the effect that members of the group who feel they have contributed toward a decision will go farther in making an effort to put it into practice than they will if it is given to them as an order from above.[2] *This tendency for the group to support a decision they have reached may be the most important consideration in judging its value.* A decision well executed may be of greater value to the organization than a better one that is only half-heartedly carried out.

There is also some evidence indicating that executives up the

[2] Norman R. F. Maier, "The Quality of Group Decisions as Influenced by the Discussion Leader," *Human Relations,* vol. 3, 1950, and other studies in Bibliography.

line to whom conference decisions are reported also tend to accept the decision or recommendation of a subordinate to a greater degree when they know it has been reached by the subordinate's (supervisor's) workers in a conference. Many executives have said that they placed high values on these reasons for holding conferences, even though they felt in some instances that they could make better decisions themselves: (1) the group's acceptance and support of its own decisions and (2) their superior's recognition of the decision arrived at by group participation.

The relationship of the amount of participation in a group to the quality of its decision is also difficult to measure. We have generally agreed that a high-participation conference is better than one with minimum discussion from the group. Stating this another way, we strive for group permissiveness and high participation rather than leader-dominated conferences. Yet we do not know that decisions reached in a maximum participation meeting are necessarily better. There is some evidence that strong, positive leaders who tend to keep the *amount* of participation down actually induce more positive, decision-reaching contributions from the group than weak leaders, as we pointed out in Chap. 6. One of our major problems in establishing principles is more one of measurement of intangibles than it is one of making sound judgments with regard to decision-making. We have said a great deal throughout the pages of this book on the *value of the combined experience, judgment, and opinion of individuals in helping to shape policy in an organization.* In a group where the experience level with the subject under discussion is high, there should be little question that decisions reached after calling on judgment and opinion based on such experience should be of high value to the organization, the leader, and the group itself.

The size of the group will have some influence on the value of its decision, with comparatively small groups best able to arrive at sound conclusions. A membership of about six to nine, with seven being an optimum number,[3] seems to be the most workable

[3] Robert F. Bales, "How People Interact in Conferences," *Scientific American,* vol. 192, March, 1955.

size. This is because a maximum amount of participation can be enjoyed by each member, a maximum amount of time can be spent on critical analysis and evaluation of proposals before the group, and differences and tensions can best be resolved. As the group gets larger and unwieldy in size, it is more difficult to get an adequate cross section of group thinking and judgment.

• *Should the decision strive for group unity or unanimity?* This question probably answers itself, for it is practically impossible to expect to reach a unanimous decision in almost any question that comes before any group. Yet both leaders and groups frequently find themselves trying to please everyone with the decision and even spending a great deal of time attempting to resolve the position of just one minority member. If such a member's support of the decision is vital to its successful execution, this may be warranted, but it is usually better to accept the fact that everyone in the group will not fully agree with the combined judgment of the entire group. The minority serves a very real and useful purpose in the decision-making process in that it helps to perfect and sharpen the decision by voicing reservations or changes. The important thing is not that the minority, regardless of its size, should be persuaded to agree with the majority so that unanimity is achieved during the decision-making process, but that it *get behind the decision and support it after it is reached, thus showing group unity to those outside the group whom the decisions will affect.*

It is not uncommon in any democratic group to find individuals and smaller internal groups expressing strong disagreement on issues that must be resolved as the decision-making process unfolds. This happens in our legislative assemblies, where members represent different political as well as personal interests, and it should be no less expected in a conference, where members come into the meeting with varied status, interests, experiences, feelings, and judgments. There is no question that there are divided loyalties and divided feelings among the members of any group. Individuals first feel the problem as it affects them individually. They also evaluate it as it relates to their work area and their own work group, and they usually defend this group and advance suggestions that will best benefit their own work group interests. Then they have loyalties to their immediate superior and to the organization as a whole. In some, loyalty to the organization may be paramount. Whether it is or is not initially, the decision-making process will be simpler and will reach more fruitful conclusions if every member of the group puts loyalty to the organization foremost (or the particular part of the work area the conference problem affects) rather than selfish interests.

• *Whose responsibility is decision-making?* The answer to this question should be obvious. But, just as many participants in a group think that it is fully the leader's responsibility to plan and carry out the purpose of a conference, they also think that the decision-making responsibility also belongs to him. Even if they want to participate in making the decision, they feel that it is his responsibility to carry it out and therefore are either half-hearted or obstructionist in helping to shape the best decision. This phase of the conference process allows for such tactics at a time when both the leader and the other members are usually anxious to draw the meeting to a close and all are interested in holding tensions and differences to a minimum. In a legislative assembly the extreme tactic to postpone a decision is the *filibuster*. In a conference this can take the form of long-winded remarks, negative and critical remarks, indifference, silence in failing to make positive remarks that would support a proposal and thus hasten a decision, poor listening throughout the conference, leading to inability to evaluate decision-making proposals properly when they are made, and otherwise failing to contribute constructively.

Decision-making is the responsibility of every member of a group, particularly when the situation is such that the group clearly understands it is free to make a decision. This responsibility should be accepted and regarded as the most valued right in the democratic process, and it behooves both leader and members to do everything they can to discharge the responsibility in the best interests of all concerned.

To summarize our considerations of the decision-making process, we can say that we all favor the democratic process, which allows for the greatest possible participation in decisions by the total group. The trend toward turning over this responsibility to subordinate levels is very much with us, as well as the trend to recognize the value of group judgment. The extent to which a decision will be made by the group will depend, however, on many factors, including the type and personality of the leader, the degree to which he has delegated the decision-making responsibility to the group, the extent to which the management of the company wants decisions made by groups as compared with supervisors, the type and objective of the particular meeting, and the group itself.

Methods of Decision-making

The actual methods used in arriving at a decision involve some of the concepts and considerations discussed above as well as the mechanics employed. Assuming a particular problem before the group, a period of time spent in its analysis, another period devoted to free offering of solutions and suggestions by the group, and following this a critical evaluation of possible solutions in order to arrive at the best solution as a basis for a decision, the leader and group are now ready to integrate their combined thinking toward the specific decision desired. This is a process of *selection, focus,* and *action.* The selection and focusing process must take place before the group is ready to indicate its decision by whatever action machinery is used.

Selection is the process of narrowing down from possibly many proposals and ideas before it the one or ones on which the group will *focus* attention. During a period of rather free discussion involving the offering of many possible solutions to a problem, individuals should not yet be thinking of the one they will ultimately accept. In considering a problem such as parking facilities at the plant, many solutions offered include these possibilities:

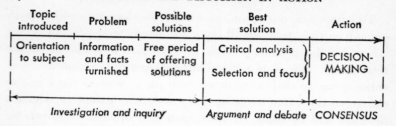

Fig. 8-1 The place of decision-making in the total discussion process.

enlarge the parking lots; change the hours for reporting to work; give parking spaces only to selected employees. The group decides to discuss first the solution to enlarge the parking lots. Actually, this process of selection involves a decision too, usually arrived at by the leader suggesting the order in which the suggestions be taken up, a member of the group suggesting the order, or some informal combination of both. The matter of selecting and narrowing down the points for focus and further discussion is important to the final decision-making of the group, for the sheer factor of time alone might preclude consideration of other items. The timing of consideration of solutions from this standpoint and from the standpoint of the mood or climate at the time attention is focused on a particular proposal may thus influence the final outcome. Individuals can influence decision-making, as can the leader, by being alert and influential in helping select and focus on one proposal as compared with another.

The *action* finally taken involves the methods or mechanics employed in finding what the judgment or will of the group is and then the way the decision will be carried out. The major question of method is the degree of informality or formality desired in getting the expression of opinion from the members of the group. The basic method used in conferences is that of *consensus,* which is the least formal method. Progressing from this to more formal procedures, the tools of *voting* and of *parliamentary procedure* may be used, though both latter methods are generally considered undesirable for conferences.

CONSENSUS

This is a much-used word in conference decision-making, generally meaning the reaching of agreement by the group, or the converging of opinion in one direction so that the total group opinion can be observed. It is difficult to suggest any specific procedure for determining the consensus of the group, for the method itself implies finding this without polling the members or asking them to vote. The leader endeavors to find the way the majority or more feel on the matter by following the trend of the discussion and taking informal note of the expressions of the members that will indicate the way opinion is shaping up. At such point when he feels he should draw the discussion to a close, and can state approximately what he thinks the group's conclusions to be, he should do so by summarizing what has been said and including in his summary the consensus as he sees it. In our discussion above under the heading "Whose decision is it?" we pointed out that this may or may not be followed by questioning the group as a whole or members individually as to their agreement with this statement. This could depend on the degree of authority in the leader, the extent to which he wants to accept fully the opinion of the group, the group's feeling of freedom to question his summary, and other things.

Consensus comes quickly where most of the members are of the same opinion. The problem then is chiefly to put their opinion into words that are satisfactory to the group. When there is a more obvious split of opinion in the group, the minority is larger and it is more difficult to achieve consensus. True consensus implies that everyone in the group will be interested in the welfare of the total group over selfish interests and that all will therefore go along with what appears to be the opinion of the majority. Although consensus does not strive for unanimity, it does involve *group unity* and the entire membership supporting the conclusion.

VOTING

Group agreement and consensus should be reached without voting in most conferences, if it is at all possible to do so. Voting tends to crystallize the pros and cons and emphasizes the majority and the minority rather than group unity. It also affords an opportunity for individuals to join forces to see if a proposal can be passed or defeated. This tends to emphasize the spirit of advocacy and contention rather than of reflective inquiry and open-mindedness that we strive for in discussion. Even though it is obvious that some are for a proposal and some are against, it is best to avoid an actual counting which will put the members into opposite camps.

Although we ideally seek consensus in a conference without voting, there are many situations and many types of meetings where it is necessary and also desirable to take a vote. In a completely permissive conference, where no formal procedures are used and there is no leader control of the outcome, it may be quite impossible to determine consensus on a particular matter before it. The leader or one of the members may therefore suggest that a vote be taken or that each person state his position openly. The latter method of going around the table for an expression from each member will indicate how the group as a whole feels on the matter and may show consensus without an actual show-of-hands vote. And if the leader or group, under unusual circumstances, feels a vote is necessary but wishes to obtain it without open indication of position, a closed vote (in writing) may be agreed upon, and the exact count need not be stated in announcing the consensus thus arrived at.

PARLIAMENTARY PROCEDURE

We have said that the use of parliamentary procedure [4] in arriving at decisions is the most formal method of group action.

[4] See the Table of Motions and the discussion of the major motions in the Appendix.

It involves a system of motions to place matters before the group for discussion, to control and facilitate discussion, and to perfect and act on all decisions. We know that legislative assemblies are run in this way, as are most business meetings of clubs and societies. The values of parliamentary procedure are that it affords an orderly method for running a meeting, it protects the rights of both majority and minority, it affords equality of participation to all members, and it expedites the handling of business. These are very desirable values in a democracy, and they are the reasons that this method is the basic method for running business meetings and legislative assemblies. But to carry out the method requires a knowledge of procedural rules and motions on the part of the leader and the members. It also imposes a degree of formality on the conduct of the discussion which does not allow for the informality, spontaneity, and permissiveness we strive for in the conference and in other types of informal discussion meetings.

Our discussion of participation in Chap. 7 pointed out that members should feel free to speak up and make contributions at any time, without recognition by the chair or first indicating their desire to speak. This allows for free and spontaneous exchange of ideas approaching the informality of conversation and inter-personal relations which is carried into the conference room. Parliamentary procedure requires recognition by the chair before speaking and also the use of motions for the introduction and amendment of any subject that is to be before the group for consideration. It also requires that decisions be reached by formal vote and counting of majority and minority. As we have pointed out, there are times when these are desirable procedures and are even quite necessary to determine the will of the majority as well as to accomplish the other values indicated.[5] But the conference-room objective is to find the will of the group while keeping group unity, as much as possible without identifying the minority, and while giving the greatest possible atmosphere for free and informal participation. While admittedly these are ideal goals

[5] See Joseph F. O'Brien, "Don't Shove, Mr. Knowles: Parliamentary Law is Basically Sound," *Today's Speech*, vol. 2, January, 1954.

which sometimes might be furthered rather than hampered by parliamentary procedure, the general tendency is not to employ the procedure in conferences.

Committee discussion comes as close to a joining of the ideals of informal and spontaneous participation and the values of parliamentary procedure, for most committees do employ procedure to some extent. We do know, however, that the committee's use of parliamentary procedure is more informal in that subjects may be discussed without first being introduced by motion, the motions ordinarily used to limit or stop debate are not employed, and other modifications are used in order to insure the greatest freedom of discussion.

Recognizing that impasses do develop in the decision-making stage of a conference when members insist on continuous argument and refuse to conciliate their opinions toward a group decision, Irving Lee has advanced a "procedure for coercing agreement" which could be invoked by the leader.[6] The procedure in brief is to prohibit any comments which are argumentative or opinionated from the time the procedure is invoked. This is to cut off further disagreement and to insist that from this point on only questions of inquiry and remarks of an informative nature or explanatory objective can be made. Having thus cooled off the atmosphere, the group then moves into decision-making in a presumably calm and reflective mood rather than an argumentative one. The procedure thus imposes a form of limit on debate similar to this motion under parliamentary procedure. It is of questionable value in that it gives somewhat authoritarian control to the leader as to when he will invoke it, it insists that points of view be withheld when they might be of value in shaping the final decision, it assumes that the group is not able to work out its discussion procedure through the normal principles and meth-

[6] For a fuller discussion of this and a reply, see Irving J. Lee, "Procedure for Coercing Agreement," *Harvard Business Review*, vol. 32, January–February, 1954, and Harold P. Zelko, "Conference Management: Beware of the Gimmicks," *Advanced Management*, vol. 19, December, 1954.

ods of good conference leadership and participation, and it imposes some rather complex mechanics of operation which may not work well unless everyone is thoroughly familiar with them.

Reaching sound decisions in a conference has no short cuts or panaceas to insure ideal results. Decision-making involves all the complex factors of individual differences, group structure and analysis, emotional involvement, thought process and reasoning, and even some of the steps in preparing which took place before the meeting started. Above all, *it requires a cooperative attitude toward accomplishing the group objective.*

INDIVIDUAL DECISION–MAKING CHECK LIST

1. Did I help toward a SYSTEMATIC DISCUSSION of the matter before us? _____
   * Following a problem-solving sequence? _____
   * Using all the steps in decision-making? _____
2. Did I approach the decision with a COOPERATIVE ATTITUDE? _____
   * After listening carefully to all? _____
   * Putting group interest above my own? _____
3. Did I CONTRIBUTE POSITIVELY to the discussion? _____
   * Refrained from making unnecessary negative comment? _____
   * Offered positive, supporting comment when I could? _____
   * Helped select and focus on major points? _____
4. Did I accept my degree of RESPONSIBILITY? _____
5. Did I SUPPORT the decision? _____
   * Go along with the consensus even though I did not originally agree? _____
   * Help present a united front? _____
   * Help put the decision into action? _____

Evaluation

Much has been learned about the group process in recent years through improved and more intense methods of evaluating what a group does. There is no question that it is well to look back and see what you did in any effort for self- or group improvement, so that you can profit from the analysis and criticism in future situations. Thus a great deal of effort has gone into the refinement of evaluation techniques. We must remember, however, that the discussion process is involved and complex and that it is far from an exact science. It therefore follows that we cannot measure it or evaluate it with exactness. A word of caution must also be inserted here regarding the evaluation process itself, which may become so involved with mechanics and measurements that we can't see the woods for the trees. The real purpose and values of the meeting should be kept in mind without allowing evaluation to get in the way.

Evaluation involves three broad areas of inquiry: (1) the achievement of the *total group goal,* (2) *individual participation* by the members, and (3) *leadership.* A sound approach should include an endeavor to find out some of these things by the time the discussion is over: Did the group accomplish its objective? How well did the members develop a group feeling of involvement and understanding of the conference objective? Was there good total participation by the group? Was participation spread among the members? Did some members contribute too much or too little? Did problems, conflicts, or tensions develop and remain unresolved? Did the discussion follow a logical and coherent sequence? Was the problem adequately analyzed? Did the leader dominate too much, or did he permit free and open discussion?

THE ROLE OF THE OBSERVER

Who does the evaluating? This question is brought to mind as we attempt to make the most of the evaluation process, which has become more and more of a special science as we try to perfect discussion methods. If evaluation is to be thorough, it is recommended that one person be appointed before the meeting starts to serve as *observer* or *recorder.* He can be a member of the group or someone not regularly associated with the group members. But if he is to be a true observer, he should not participate in the actual discussion, and he should spend all of his time listening and recording, in as detached an attitude as possible.

The value of the observer is very high in experimental work on the conference and discussion process, where he should be a trained expert in the process if he is to be thorough. In the average meeting, however, any member of a group may detach himself for a particular meeting as observer and do a satisfactory job. The practice of rotating this role among the group members is a good one in regularly scheduled groups, for the conference participant who finds himself as an observer develops a new perspective and an analytical approach to conference techniques that will be helpful to him when he returns to his role as participant.

Although the designation of a particular individual as observer is helpful to sharpen the evaluation, a great deal of good can come from the group's own self-evaluation in which all the members and the chairman hold a *postmeeting discussion* of what happened during the actual conference or discussion program. Such a discussion may be joined in by all those present, as well as the chairman. As members enter into the spirit of talking about each other and offering constructive criticism and suggestions, there is a mutual benefit to all concerned that will show up to advantage in future meetings. An *observer team* of two to four members of the group may be designated in advance to come forward and discuss the meeting as a panel, as another means of getting member participation in the observer role.

Feedback is the term applied to the process of communicating back to the group the observations made as to their conduct of the discussion during the meeting itself. Normally, it includes what the observer tells the group he observed during the discussion, but we also use the term broadly to apply to what is said by anyone who participates in a postmeeting evaluation. The point is that the group is now being "fed back" what it originally said and did so that it now gets a clear picture, in retrospect, of what happened. This is most effective when it is not a one-way street from observer or critic back to the group, but rather when there is open and free exchange and questions to clarify in everyone's mind the points and techniques being evaluated.

Feedback is most effective when it is organized systematically around specific areas of evaluation and does not skip around haphazardly. This might be a suggested pattern:

- How well did the *group* accomplish its broad objectives?
- Did the *leader* do a good job?
- Was there good *participation?*
- Were there any *difficult situations?*
- How about the *facilities?*

Record-keeping may be part of the observer's job, and the discussion of this in Chap. 5 may be reviewed in this connection.

MEASUREMENT AND EVALUATION METHODS

Evaluation will be most effective if it is approached with specific objectives in mind and if certain methods and tools are used to facilitate the process. A true observer is technique- and methods-minded, and he should not reflect on the problem, the issues, or the pros and cons of the discussion as it unfolds. He should concentrate on *how* all this is being done: how well, how poorly, how much, how little, and how fundamental leadership and discussion methods are employed. He is concerned with *measuring* and *evaluating,* with measurement taking place before evaluation.

Measurement is primarily a matter of recording what goes on, and most of the tools devised for this purpose in the form of sociograms, charts, check lists, and evaluation sheets are chiefly to help simplify the recording process. It is much easier to record *quantity* than *quality* of discussion, both of which we are concerned with in evaluation. We can record the number of times an individual participated, and this may be meaningful, but a few contributions of high quality might be more productive to the conference goal than many remarks of less substance. Another factor still harder to measure by recording is the *exchange* and *interrelationships* among the participants, with the sociogram and its variants being the chief tool for doing this. We are therefore interested in quantity, quality, and relationships in the measurement process.

Interpreting all that we have observed and measured and recorded is the specific process of evaluation. And to make the task even more difficult, we must remember that we are evaluating at least three things that are all interrelated: the leader, the group, and the participants.

The *sociogram* type of chart and its variants attempt to record the participation by each member and its relation to the other members. It is the relationship among the members that is the significant value of this kind of observation and recording. The typical chart starts with a blank diagram of the conference table showing the position of each member. As each contribution is made, this is recorded by an arrow and by additional coding techniques that might indicate the type of remark (such as question, information-giving, reply, offering opinion). Such a recording system is feasible in a group up to ten, although even this size becomes difficult to record as the discussion progresses. Two suggested forms are indicated in Fig. 8-2. It should be remembered that the recording is only as good as its interpretation, and it is perhaps better to record fewer items clearly than to try to record everything that happens and not be able to decipher the recordings.

If the group does not number more than about six members, the form of recording in Fig. 8-3 may be clearer to interpret and also may facilitate the recording process. It has the advantage over the typical sociogram forms in that the space problem does not become complicated when there is a long exchange between two members, since the recorder simply moves across the page

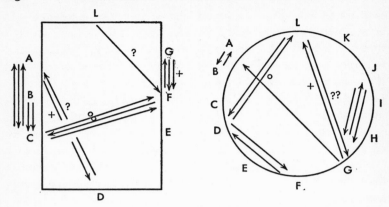

?	Overhead or general question
??	Direct question
+	Offers information
o	Offers opinion

Fig. 8-2 Typical recordings of discussion.

and can use another sheet if this space runs out. The leader and participants are placed in a line at the left in order of their seating at the table.

In this discussion it can be noted that C was the most active participant, having engaged in exchanges expressing opinion with B, D, and E. Otherwise the discussion was fairly well spread, except for A, who contributed only twice, once in response to a question. The leader did not dominate or control the discussion very much, having spoken four times after he got it started with a general or overhead question. The exchanges between C and other individuals could be analyzed further to see the extent of the conflicts and their effect on the total participation of the group.

When observation cannot be as specific as charting every contribution in a discussion, the evaluator or observer may use a check list or evaluation form. A number of such suggested forms for various kinds of discussion meetings and programs are on the

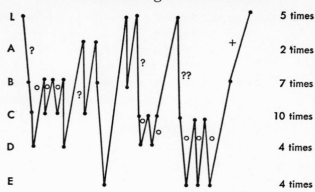

Fig. 8-3   Chart form for recording discussion.

following pages. It would be impractical to have a form for every different type of meeting, and some of the forms may be used for various purposes.

Form A. Conference Evaluation

This could be used for all types of single-meeting conferences. The bottom part of the form, showing a line for each member, can be used either to rate the member or to chart the participation from one to another as in the diagram above. All of the items listed on the form may be rated, or comment may be written in on the line. This form could also be used for panel and committee discussion.

Form B. Public Discussion Program Evaluation

This form does not differ materially from Form A but contains some items not looked for in a conference. If used for a symposium or debate, each speaker may be rated separately.

Form C. Conference Program Evaluation

This is suggested for longer conferences or convention programs that comprise a number of smaller or sectional meetings, also for workshop-type programs. Form A should be used for evaluating each separate meeting.

Form D. Participant's Check List

This might be used to count the number of contributions each member made in each type of remark during the discussion.

Form E. Individual Reaction Sheet

Each member of the group would use this sheet to check his own participation and reaction to the discussion as a type of self-evaluation.

Form F. Interview Evaluation

This form would be used for evaluating an interview and would be most useful in an interview training program either for sales, counseling, employment, or other type of interview objective.

A   **CONFERENCE EVALUATION FORM**
(For evaluating most conferences)

Subject ———————————— Leader ———————— Date ———

	VERY GOOD	GOOD	FAIR
Planning			
Facilities			
THE LEADER (total rating)			
Opening remarks			
Agenda, problem, or topic stated			
Stimulated discussion			
Controlled discussion			
Use of questions			
Use of charts and blackboard			
Use of cases and handouts			
Transitions			
Summary			
Pleasant manner			
Tact			
Impartial			
THE GROUP (total rating)			
Problem discussed			
Facts and information supplied			
Solutions advanced			
Solutions discussed and evaluated			
Decision-making and consensus			
Cooperative attitude			
PARTICIPATION (total rating)			
Member A			
Member B			
Etc.			
TOTAL CONFERENCE RATING			

B   PUBLIC DISCUSSION PROGRAM EVALUATION FORM
(For evaluating most panel, symposium, and group discussion programs)

Subject ———————— Leader ———— Date ————

	VERY GOOD	GOOD	FAIR
Planning			
Facilities			
THE LEADER (total rating)			
Opening remarks			
Introductions			
Conduct of discussion			
Visual aids			
Transitions			
Summary			
Conduct of forum period			
Manner and speaking			
THE GROUP (total rating)			
Integrated discussion			
Spontaneous			
Problem discussed			
Solutions advanced			
Solutions discussed and evaluated			
Conclusions			
Cooperative attitude			
THE PARTICIPANTS (rate each one)			
A			
B			
C			
D			
TOTAL PROGRAM RATING			

C   CONFERENCE PROGRAM EVALUATION FORM
(For multimeeting programs, conventions, and workshops)

Name of conference ———————————————————————

Place ——————————————————————— Date ———————————

ARRANGEMENTS

    Meeting rooms:

    Housing:

    Meals:

    Other:

PROGRAM

    General plan of conference:

    Subjects covered:

    Sectional meetings and programs:

      Speakers:

        Contributed most (why):

        Contributed least (why):

    Group participation:

OTHER MATTERS OR SUGGESTIONS

(Use reverse side for further comment)

D   **PARTICIPANTS CHECK LIST**

(For recording type and amount of participation)

CONTRIBUTION	A	B	C	D	E	F	G	H	I
Asks for information									
Asks for suggestions									
Asks for opinion									
Offers information									
Offers explanation									
Offers opinion									
Supporting									
Opposing									
Argues—shows tension									
Suggests agenda topic									
Makes transition									
Makes summary									
Seeks to make decision									

E   **INDIVIDUAL REACTION SHEET**
(For individual member self-analysis)

	YES	PARTLY	NO
Was this a *worthwhile meeting?*			
Was the *objective accomplished?*			
Was the meeting *well planned?*			
Did the *leader* do a good job?			
Did the leader *dominate* too much?			
Did I feel *free to contribute?*			
Did I *supply information* when I could?			
Did I have a *cooperative attitude?*			
Did I have an *open mind?*			
Was my *interest* maintained?			
Was I a *good listener?*			
Did I *speak appropriately?*			
Did I help keep the *discussion organized?*			
Should I have *prepared more?*			
Did I help toward *reaching a decision?*			

F   **INTERVIEW EVALUATION FORM**

Interviewer ——————— Interviewee ——————— Date ———

Purpose ————————————————————————————

INTERVIEWING STEPS   VERY GOOD   GOOD   FAIR

Greeting and opening ——————————————————

Interest aroused ——————————————————————

Need or problem ————————————————————————

Information obtained ——————————————————————

Solution or presentation ——————————————————

Demonstration ——————————————————————————

Action or close ——————————————————————————

INTERVIEW CONDUCT

Adaptation to interviewee ——————————————————

Common ground ————————————————————————

Use of questions ——————————————————————

Facts and supporting material ————————————————

Appeal to motives ——————————————————————

INTERVIEW MANNER

Attitude ————————————————————————————

Physical bearing ——————————————————————

Tact and diplomacy ——————————————————————

Speaking ——————————————————————————————

Listening ——————————————————————————————

MEETING OBJECTIONS AND ANSWERING QUESTIONS

1.

2.

3.

INTERVIEWER'S TOTAL RATING——————————————

Conclusion

Reaching decisions through discussion is the true democratic goal of the discussion process. The achievement of the goal to the satisfaction of a group will depend on the use that is made of most of the principles, methods, and suggestions made thus far in this book. This chapter has attempted to bring together the more specific process of decision-making itself and its relation to the total discussion process. We should keep in mind whose decision we are seeking, how good a decision we can reach, and the responsibility of all members of a group in achieving unity. Selection and focus are necessary steps prior to action on a decision. Consensus is the chief goal and the major method, with voting and use of parliamentary procedure infrequently used in conferences. Cooperation of all in supporting a decision is essential.

Evaluating discussion is becoming more and more recognized as a major tool for improving leadership and participation. The observer role and the use of the entire group for self-evaluation should be employed to the extent that time and the occasion permit. There are many tools for measuring and evaluating discussion, both in terms of quantity and quality and of interrelationships. Evaluation is a difficult process because of the complexity of discussion itself and because of the many things we are trying to perfect, including the leader, the participants, and the group. Forms and check lists will make the job easier. Probably the chief benefit from evaluation is in the postmeeting feedback and discussion by the group of its own activities during the meeting itself.

APPLYING THIS CHAPTER

1. The next time you attend a conference, make a chart of the flow of participation, the amount and kind of participation of each member, and an evaluation of the total conference participation.

2. Make a critical and thorough analysis of the leadership of a conference. Analyze your own good and bad practices as a leader.

3. Encourage an evaluation session after your next conference. Then get the group to assess the value of such a postconference evaluation session.

4. In a social conversational situation, observe the trend in the discussion as to whether the group converged toward consensus or agreement. Does such a social group usually try to reach consensus? What part can a group member play in trying to bring this about?

5. Analyze the reasons why it is best not to take votes in order to reach decisions in a conference.

6. Prepare a five-minute feedback report on a conference where you have had the role of observer. What values are there in appointing an observer in advance of the conference rather than having a participant (or the whole group) serve this function?

IV

THE NATURE OF
PUBLIC DISCUSSION

Having considered the total place of discussion in society, the principles and methods applicable to all discussion, and the particular application of these to the conference, we now turn our attention to public discussion situations. Keeping in mind that most of what we have said up to now is applicable, we are concerned with an understanding and analysis of the types of public discussion and how they differ from private conference. Then we are concerned with the application of discussion principles to planning, preparing, leading, and participating in public discussion programs.

CHAPTER 9

Types and Patterns
of Public Discussion

WE HAVE ALREADY pointed out that discussion methods do not change materially in going from one group situation to another. We have also distinguished public from private discussion in that the former takes place before an audience of nonparticipants until the "program" aspect of the discussion is finished, after which they are brought into participation in what is usually called a *forum period*. Since the term "public discussion" is generally applied to all meetings where some sort of presentation is made in front of the total group by one or more persons, the forms or types of such presentations vary considerably. This variation tends to be in the nature of a progression from informal to formal, the panel being the most informal and the lecture or debate being the most formal.

We are also including "group discussion" as public discussion because the term is usually applied in meetings of a public nature, yet it is also applied to all situations involving the discussion process, as we pointed out in Chap. 2.

The Nature of Public Discussion

Public discussion, then, is exceedingly broad and varied and is made up of a wide number of situations that one confronts in the social and political life of a democracy. It includes political rallies addressed by speakers, where there is little audience participation besides cheers and flag-waving. It includes the discussion of a public issue by members of a panel on television or radio, such as the *Meet the Press* program, where the discussion takes place before us and we participate as silent observers. It includes the lecture by a professor who leaves time for just one question by the class before the period is up. All of these situations allow for little or no actual talking participation by the audience, yet many of us would call them "discussion meetings."

More typically of what we like to feel is true public discussion, where the total audience participates more, would be a club or lodge meeting; a P.-T.A. meeting, where all present enter into the discussion of all matters coming before the group, a classroom where the teacher poses questions and otherwise stimulates the class to participate in true group discussion of the subject for that period; a legislative assembly, where everyone present has an equal voice and opportunity to participate, which is one of the values of parliamentary procedure, since it insures equal opportunity; a lively panel discussion of three or four people who stimulate the thinking of the larger audience, which is then given ample time to raise questions and make comments for full participation.

In other words, there is so much variety of both types of meetings and opportunity for and amount of participation by the total group that our definition of the nature of public discussion must be a very fluid one. We can all agree that the goal is a proper relationship between the program held in front of the group and the participation of the group itself. But there is no exact formula for what this relationship should be ideally. In one situation, the objective is accomplished fully by stimulating the thinking of the larger group without any actual vocal participation of the group. In another they should be given the full time of the meeting for their participation. As we examine the various types of public discussion meetings, we can keep this question before us.

Types of Public Discussion Meetings

Group	Debate-forum
Forum	Lecture-forum
Panel-forum	Radio and
Symposium-forum	television programs

GROUP

Group discussion is the exchange of information, opinion, and ideas among all members of a group. It is usually regarded as embracing the participation of the entire group, although, as we have just pointed out, the extent of this varies considerably. When a number of people come together (preferably fewer than twenty, if true group discussion is to take place) for some purpose and proceed to talk among themselves, they are participating in group discussion. This can be in the nature of *informal conversation,* as friends come together for the *pleasure* of each other's company. Or the purpose, as in a club meeting, might be to *arrive at a decision* whether to contribute five dollars or fifty dollars to the Community Chest. The purpose of the gathering will not determine whether group discussion takes place as much as will the type of program or the method of leadership employed, as was discussed in Chap. 2.

The nature and extent of the discussion by the group depends a great deal on how it is started. In a conference or a committee or in a small learning group such as a class, a leader is present who may use a variety of methods and techniques for stimulating and guiding discussion, as we pointed out in Chap. 6. In informal conversation, and sometimes in very informal round-table discussions, there may be no leader to get the discussion started or to guide it. In these situations, members of the group assume leadership functions and one member may emerge as the leader; in all of them the discussion is started and motivated within the group itself.

FORUM

A *forum is the participation of the entire group after a planned program of discussion (or lecture) has been held and the balance of the time is turned over to the group for questions, comments, and exchange of ideas.* The forum discussion is thus motivated initially by the discussion which takes place in front of the larger group. The exchange is usually between members of the group and the participants in the planned program up front, although an exchange among group members themselves frequently takes place. This may be explained by the chairman before the forum starts, as we point out in Chap. 11. Almost all the discussion types described below are followed by such a forum in order to allow for audience participation. Programs such as the panel, symposium, debate, and lecture, and such techniques as role-playing and the analysis of cases serve largely as a background for stimulating group thinking and later participation. The primary purpose of a forum is educational and instructive.

THE PANEL-FORUM

A *panel discussion is an exchange of thought and ideas among several participants, usually three to five, in the nature of informal but organized conversation, in front of a larger listening group.* In most panel programs,[1] the larger group enters into the discussion as the forum part of the program, after about thirty to forty minutes of discussion by the panel itself.

If a panel discussion is held in a room without a larger audience, this would be a conference or committee discussion. The

---

[1] We have used the word "program" to describe this kind of discussion, for usually any discussion of a small number before a larger group is regarded as a program for the benefit of the larger group. This is another distinguishing feature between public and private discussion, for we never regard a true conference as a program in this sense.

term "panel" is used rather loosely to describe a small discussion group of any sort. This is why we refer to a "panel of speakers" at a meeting where the nature of the program is really a series of individual talks, or a symposium. But this is of course not a true panel discussion, which by definition is always an informal and spontaneous exchange among the participants, with no prepared formal talks.

The terms "round table" and "colloquy" are frequently used to describe types of programs quite similar to the panel. The *round table,* however, is usually a private discussion group seated face to face around a table, without a larger audience. It is a small conference by another name. The *colloquy* is a public type of discussion program in the nature of a panel, but it gets its peculiar name from the participants and objective sought in the discussion. The colloquy brings the panel members before the larger group, along with experts on the subject who may be invited to sit with the panel and who may come from the larger group or from the outside. They are sometimes seated at a separate table with the chairman in the center and the regular panel members at another table.

THE SYMPOSIUM-FORUM

A symposium discussion is an exchange of thought among several participants, usually three or four, to a larger audience, in the nature of prepared formal talks made by each participant on some phase of the general topic. The symposium is thus more formal than the panel, with each of the speeches usually presented from the center of the platform with the speaker standing as in a formal speech. This is still regarded by most people as a discussion program in that the talks by each participant are related and should represent an exchange of ideas among the participants. To accomplish this, although the major part of each talk is prepared in advance, the speaker should leave part of his time for the informal exchange and adaptation to other talks in order to achieve the desired exchange and this characteristic of discussion. In this sense the symposium participant should come into the meeting with an open mind and an attitude of inquiry and reflective thinking which are regarded as part of the discussion process, even though he prepares a talk representing a particular point of view in advance. The plan or sequence of the speeches in a symposium usually follows a continuity pattern from a discussion and analysis of the problem by the first speaker, followed by different solutions or different views on the same solution by succeeding speakers. A symposium may also follow a purely informational or instructional sequence in which all of the speakers contribute to the analysis of a problem or to the information, facts, or explanation to be presented. In such a program on a topic as "The Many Uses of Atomic Energy," speaker A might talk on "History of Atomic Energy," speaker B on "The Atomic Bomb," speaker C on "Other Atomic Weapons," and speaker D on "Peacetime Uses of Atomic Energy." The symposium thus becomes an educational medium, rather than one for the discussion or solution to a problem such as "How can we control the atom bomb?" which is the type of topic more commonly used.

THE DEBATE-FORUM

A debate is an exchange of thought and argument by persons on opposing sides of a proposition or question. Usually there are two persons on each side, and they are directly opposed to the point of view represented by the other side. Debate, therefore, is not discussion in the true sense, for there is no attitude of inquiry and reflective thinking as to what is the best solution. The debater has made up his mind in advance, and he does all he can to advance and defend his own point of view with no thought to being "won over" by his opposition. The term "opposition" is quite common to debate, as is the concept of the other side being represented by "opponents." The good discussion participant never regards other participants as opponents even though he may be in disagreement with their points of view from time to time as the discussion progresses.

Nevertheless, debate is usually considered as a type of discussion program in that it does represent a method for discussing a *controversial* subject before an audience. We may also consider debate as the later stage of a continuum in the discussion process which is reached in most problem-solving discussions after the problem is analyzed and solutions proposed. During these earlier steps in discussion, participants are rarely in conflict, and the attitude is one of inquiry. Then as particular solutions and proposals are considered, deliberated, and weighed, individuals tend to advance and defend their points of view, sides may be taken, and argument and advocacy are evident. If we consider the discussion process to be the entire exchange among the participants from the time the meeting opens until decisions are reached at the end, debate is a part of the whole process.

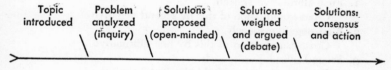

Fig. 9-1   Discussion-debate continuum.

From the standpoint of debate as a type of discussion program, which is our chief interest at this point, it is one of the more formal types in which each participant makes a prepared speech for or against the proposition.[2] Speakers alternate on the affirmative side and negative side, with the affirmative starting and closing the debate. The length of speeches may vary considerably, with a typical debate taking a total of forty to sixty minutes. In

[2] The wording of debate propositions is discussed more fully under consideration of Topics in Chap. 10.

formal college debate, all speakers usually give a rebuttal speech, but one rebuttal on each side is sometimes the case in a shorter program. The "orthodox" debate proceeds like this:

First affirmative speaker—10 min
First negative speaker—10 min
Second affirmative speaker—10 min
Second negative speaker—10 min
First negative rebuttal—5 min
First affirmative rebuttal—5 min
Second negative rebuttal—5 min
Second affirmative rebuttal—5 min

There are many variants of this, one of the chief forms being the cross-examination debate, in which members of each side ask questions of the speakers on the opposite side as the debate progresses. This lends a lively touch to the discussion and is usually of interest to the listening audience. The number of cross-examination periods and the final summary speeches may vary, with the typical sequence going like this:

1. First affirmative speech
   Cross-examination of this by second negative
2. First negative speech
   Cross-examination of this by first affirmative
3. Second affirmative speech
   Cross-examination of this by first negative
4. Second negative speech
   Cross-examination of this by second affirmative
5. Summary and refutation by negative
6. Summary and refutation by affirmative

THE LECTURE-FORUM

This is considered as a discussion program only in that the audience is given a chance to participate after the lecture is finished. It is a single speech, usually occupying most of the time of the meeting, followed by a question-and-answer period. In most formal lecture situations, the participation by the audience is limited to questions asked of the speaker. Sometimes the speech is planned to be comparatively short in relation to the total time of the meeting, in which case it is used chiefly as a background to stimulate the thinking of the audience, and there is then considerably more audience participation. The average lecture in a classroom should be planned with time left for questions. But the habits and methods of the lecturer usually set the pattern that the discussion will take. In public lectures, this should be planned between the speaker and the chairman.

RADIO AND TELEVISION PROGRAMS

Radio and television provide the medium and setting for a variety of types of discussion programs, that may take any of the above forms. Probably the *panel* is the most common type of program, since it embodies the qualities of informality and spontaneity that will best hold the interest of an unseen listening audience. Programs like the *University of Chicago Round Table* and *Meet the Press* are among the best-known radio and television discussion programs using largely the panel as the basic type of discussion. The former is closest to the typical panel form, though *Meet the Press* has a different format in that it brings an expert or public figure as the key member of the panel, who is interviewed in turn by the other panel members.

The *interview* is a commonly used medium for both radio and television, in news broadcasts and special programs to stimulate audience interest on particular subjects. The *symposium* is used occasionally, with the formal *debate* as the least frequently used. *Town Meeting of the Air* has a format which usually presents three or four speeches by individuals presenting different points of view on a common topic. Occasionally, this program will have two speakers on each side of a question and will be quite similar to formal debate.

A number of problems come into the picture when any type of discussion program is presented on radio or television. In radio,

the time limit is very strict and must be planned for; the invisible
audience demands attention in matters such as voice, articulation,
and language; and the psychological factor of not seeing the
audience sometimes creates a mental barrier for the participant.
Audience participation as a forum is eliminated, yet the panel
participants must always be conscious that they are speaking to
a live audience. In television, much the same problems exist except that a live audience is usually in the studio. Television speaking, in most program situations, is for the benefit of the larger
viewing audience not in the studio. The speaking and participating must be lively. The problem of notes concerns most television
speakers in that they should not be in obvious view of the audience.
Mechanical prompters are available for major television presentations, but the average person should rely on his own preparation.
Printed material on large cards not seen by the television audience may be helpful. Participants may use notes if they are careful
not to look down at them too frequently and if they are familiar
with them.

Visual aids are of great help to any television program, and for
the average speaker the prepared chart is probably the most
useful type of aid. Objects, models, and other devices on which
the camera can focus will also be helpful.

Perhaps the most important visual part of the television presentation is the facial expression of the participants. Sincerity,
enthusiasm, and constant interest must be displayed in both face
and posture.

Preparation and participation in both radio and television discussion programs should include all the steps, suggestions, and
methods we have pointed out for the successful execution of these
programs in any medium.

The Discussion Pattern

Since public discussion is largely a problem-solving process, the
sequence pattern for almost all of the types of programs and

meetings follows the normal thought process of reflective thinking as we discussed this in Chap. 4. Whether planning for a panel,
symposium, or general group discussion, the chairman would normally guide the discussion through an analysis of the problem,
possible solutions, best solution, and recommended action. In a
debate the speakers also tend to follow this pattern, although they
will argue more about the extent of the problem and then con-
verge their argument on the pros and cons of a particular solution.
Even the lecturer's speech should follow through this sequence.
It should be remembered that most public discussions do not
reach decisions; hence the best solution and action steps may not
be completed.

Various subjects and situations also call for different degrees
of emphasis on the problem or solution phase of a discussion. In
one situation, the group may be concerned primarily with the
extent or the seriousness of the problem; in another, such as in a
learning situation, the problem may be assumed or accepted, and
the group will spend most of its time discussing and explaining
different plans or principles or methods (solutions). The discussion pattern, then, is related to the basic purpose to be accomplished in the meeting.

The attitude of inquiry which should prevail in discussion is
reflected in the outline [3] on pp. 182–183 of the typical discussion
pattern in the form of *questions to be raised* rather than direct
statements of main points to be covered.

Conclusion

Public discussion usually involves a program in which a small
number of persons discuss a topic or question before a larger
listening audience. Such programs fall into several types such as
the panel, symposium, and debate, all of which may be followed
by a period of audience participation or forum. The panel is the

[3] An outline for an actual discussion program and topic is found in
Chap. 10.

most informal and spontaneous form and is also the form that most nearly approximates true discussion among the participants, as in a conference. The symposium presents prepared speeches by the participants, as do the debate and the lecture-forum, although the latter two types are not strictly discussion in that the speakers present points of view and argument rather than inquire as to the best solution.

All discussion tends to follow a basic problem-solution pattern which should be carefully thought through by both chairman and participants before the meeting. The degree of emphasis on any particular step in the pattern will depend on the topic and the purpose the group wants to accomplish from the discussion.

TYPICAL DISCUSSION OUTLINE PATTERN

INTRODUCTION

Attention

I. Chairman's opening remarks
  A. Greeting
  B. Introduction of participants
  C. Statement of topic or question

MAIN DISCUSSION

Problem

I. What is the problem out of which this question grows?
  A. How serious is it today?
    1. Whom does it affect?
    2. Where is it?
    3. How much does it cost?
  B. When and how did this condition start?
    4. How long has it been with us?
    5. What are the causes?
  C. Is the total problem clear to all of us?
    1. Are there any ambiguous terms?
    2. Should we raise other questions?

Possible solutions

II. What are the possible solutions and suggestions?
  A. Can we list all suggestions before discussing them?

B. Have we overlooked any possibilities?
C. What are the values of each solution? Disadvantages?
   1. Will it solve the problem?
   2. Remove the causes?
   3. Be practical?
   4. Bring new evils?

The solution

III. What is the best solution? (may emerge from II, C)
A. What goals are we seeking?
B. Is there one solution that seems to meet these goals?
C. Can we agree on this solution? (consensus)
D. Should we make only tentative recommendations?

Action

IV. What action should be taken?
A. Are we ready to recommend a specific plan?
   1. How will it be carried out?
   2. Who will do it?
B. Should we postpone specific action?

CONCLUSION (OR FORUM PERIOD)

I. Summary and transition remarks by chairman
II. Questions and comments from listening group
   A. Addressed to chair or individual participant
   B. Addressed to participants as a whole
III. Final summary and remarks by chairman

APPLYING THIS CHAPTER

1. Look back on the last lecture you attended. Could this have been made more interesting as a panel or symposium program with several participants?
2. Analyze a radio or television discussion program you have heard recently. Does it fit into any of the specific types of public discussion?
3. Try to attend a college debate and note how this differs from the typical problem-solving process of a good conference.

4. Do you feel that the panel or the symposium is more difficult for a leader to run? What methods can you employ to encourage the more informal and spontaneous exchange that is sometimes difficult to achieve in a panel?
5. Do you think the typical discussion pattern can be applied fully to all discussion programs?

CHAPTER 10

Planning for Discussion Programs

THE FOUR PARTICIPANTS who had been invited to be members of a panel at the monthly meeting of the local chapter of the Business and Professional Women's Club arrived from different directions and confronted each other with a combination of worried looks. They were asked to discuss the subject of "Safe Driving in the Community" by the program chairman who told them to come a little bit early and get further instructions from the person who would be chairman of the panel. Participants A and B had notes in their pockets for prepared speeches, A's being about five minutes long and B's about fifteen minutes. Participants C and D had done some thinking about the subject and had come prepared to talk it over informally as a panel and with no speeches. None of the four knew the length of the program or whether there would be a forum period for questions and answers after their part of the program was finished. The chairman finally arrived and was somewhat perplexed over this state of affairs, insisting that the panel members were just to say a few words in turn on the subject. Since the time for the program had arrived, C and D hastily put together some impromptu remarks for short speeches, and A and B tried to adjust the length of their prepared talks to the approximate length of talk that was wanted. They floundered through a discussion that was a cross between a symposium and a panel, and a good job of neither.

Unfortunately, this is far too typical of the type of planning that is done for discussion programs. Individuals are asked to participate without proper understanding and directions, and programs are thrown together haphazardly. Good programs don't just happen; they are the result of planning by those responsible for setting them up and of preparation by those who are to participate. The program chairman of an organization has a long-range job of planning a series of meetings, perhaps over a period of a year. He should try to have variety in subjects, participants, and types of programs. And in regard to each one he should insure that all of the steps in the planning process are carried out, either by himself or the chairman of the particular program.

STEPS IN DISCUSSION PROGRAM PLANNING

1. Determine the *nature of the meeting and group*.
2. Determine the best *type of discussion*.
3. Select and word the *topic*.
4. Select and *notify the participants*.
5. Hold a *planning meeting* with the participants.
6. Arrange *facilities*.
7. Study the *subject*.
8. Prepare a *discussion outline* for the whole program.
9. Prepare a *speech outline* (if making a speech as a participant).
10. Consider what *publicity* is needed.

1. *Determine the nature of the meeting and group.* In planning a series of programs for a particular group, the basic purpose and interest of the group would influence the choice of subject and participants. The meeting place might influence the type of program best suitable to the facilities at hand. The presence of certain members of the group might influence the appropriateness of certain subjects and points of view. Regardless of the characteristics of a group, the discussion program should be planned for the most possible stimulation and interest of the group members.

It is best to weigh carefully the subjects under consideration and the available participants before making a final decision, with the best interest of the maximum number of group members in mind.

2. *Determine the best type of discussion.* This is a question whether a panel, symposium, or lecture-forum might be best for the particular subject and occasion. The program planner should know the difference between the basic types and the advantages of each. Some public programs in a community, such as a local town meeting or public forum, may have a regular format which is already determined for the program planner. This is true of many radio and television programs that are repeated at regular intervals. But if this is not the case, certain considerations may influence the type of program selected. If there is an outstanding speaker available for a particular meeting, this may be good reason for planning a lecture-forum. If the subject under discussion is highly controversial and subject to considerable analysis and many points of view, a panel will stimulate lively thinking and interest. If a problem or new plan is complex and requires a great deal of factual information for proper understanding, a symposium of experts supplying the necessary facts or explanation may be most desirable. If there seem to be just two sides to a particular issue, a debate should be most fruitful.

In other words, there are logical reasons for selecting a certain type of program for a certain group and subject, or with particular participants in mind. As indicated in our example of the poorly planned program, it is important that both chairman and participants understand in advance what type of program they should plan for.

3. *Select and word the topic.* This may be done before step 2, where a group decides that it would like to hear (or participate in) a certain topic, and then all the planning is done to carry out this decision. Actually, the steps we are enumerating in planning for discussion need not necessarily be taken up in this order. A planning meeting of all participants may be the first step when

the type of program and topic wording should be decided upon.

Selection of the topic may grow out of the particular interests of the group, the current timeliness of certain issues, the availability of speakers, or other interests of those planning the program. In a civic-minded group, community issues such as schools, roads, traffic problems, juvenile delinquency, and taxes would be of interest. Topics of world and political affairs, such as communism, the atom bomb, and the United Nations are of interest to most mature groups. On a college campus, other issues such as student regulations, examinations, and fraternities might be proposed as discussion topics.

Having selected the topic or subject area for the discussion, the next important step is to word it so that it will provoke interest. In the true spirit of a discussion attitude of inquiry, the topic should be worded as a question. Words like "how" and "what" at the beginning of the question will provoke interest, such as "How can we solve the traffic problem in our community?" But this topic wording may be too broad, and this brings us to another suggestion. The topic should be stated to indicate the probable scope of the discussion and should be kept within comparatively narrow limits. This topic would be narrower by confining it to the "parking" rather than the "traffic" problem, thus reading "How can we solve the parking problem in our community?" Using the word "what" to introduce this topic, we could word it as "What can we do about the parking problem?"

The discussion topic as a rule should avoid posing one solution which will be argued pro and con unless a debate is being planned. The wordings we have just suggested would leave the door wide open for possible solutions by the participants; but a wording such as "Should the community build a downtown parking lot?" might not. This would imply that the discussion would enter the debate stage, after analyzing the parking problem, in which speakers would be for or against the building of such a lot. The debate of course does not preclude speakers suggesting alternate solutions to the one in the question, but this is somewhat different from the free offering of possible solutions in a true discussion.

The statement of the topic for debate is frequently called the debate *proposition*. In formal debate it is stated as a *resolution,* such as "Resolved, that we should build a downtown community parking lot." The debate topic should avoid ambiguous words and terms, so that both sides will interpret the terms in the same way. Yet defining the terms in the question is frequently the first step in the actual discussion by the first debate speaker. The wording should also make clear the position and proposal the affirmative side will have to uphold.

Summarizing these suggestions for the discussion topic wording:

* It should be stated as a question.
* Words such as "how" and "what" stimulate interest.
* The question raised should not be too broad.
* The topic statement should use a minimum number of words.
* For debate, the proposal should be clear, language should not be ambiguous, and the question should be in the affirmative.

Using some of the subjects indicated above, here are suggested topic wordings:

SUBJECT	DISCUSSION TOPIC	DEBATE TOPIC
Downtown parking	How can we solve the downtown parking problem in our community?	Should our community build a downtown parking lot?
Schools	What should we do about over-crowded classes?	Resolved, that we should limit all classes to twenty students.
	How can we improve teacher's salaries?	Should we impose a special tax levy to be used for increasing teacher's salaries?
Communism	What is the best way to get along with Russia?	Resolved, that we abolish diplomatic relations with Russia.

| Atom bomb | How can the atom bomb be controlled? | Should the U.S. stop making experimental tests of the atom bomb? |
| Juvenile delinquency | What are the answers to the juvenile delinquency problem? | Should our city impose a curfew on minors under 16? |

4. *Select the participants and notify them.* In arranging for participants in a discussion program, a major consideration is that they come from different backgrounds and with different experiences so that they are likely to have an exchange of ideas, information, and points of view. Keeping in mind that discussion is the exchange and pooling together of the thoughts and experiences of the participants, the sum total will represent a richer accumulation of ideas and conclusions if the participants do not all think alike at the outset. In the panel or general group discussion situation, the way in which varied points of view will be expressed and related to each other by the various participants will make for a desired exchange of ideas. In the symposium or debate, participants should be selected with this question in mind to insure that different solutions are offered (in the symposium) or that both sides are represented (in the debate).

When an individual is invited to participate in a discussion program, he should be given the feeling that this is looked upon by you and your organization as an important event. He should be asked well in advance of the program date, and preferably by letter. Then, after the meeting has been held, a letter of thanks should be sent. Either in the letter of invitation, or by telephone, he should be given all the details needed, including the time, place, exact wording of the question, the length of the program, just what you want him to do, whether there will be a forum period, the nature and purpose of the group, and the names of other panel participants. Assuming that there will be a planning meeting with all the participants, some of this information might be discussed at the meeting. If a planning meeting is not possible, a personal contact with each participant should be made, particularly to arrive at a clear understanding of the part he will play in the program.

5. *Hold a planning meeting with the participants.* This is the best way to insure a successful program. The main purpose of a preliminary meeting is to discuss the ways and means for carrying out the program, not to rehearse the discussion. Ordinarily it is unnecessary, and even unwise, to rehearse the discussion, particularly for a panel, for this takes away the lively spontaneity that is so desirable. The planning meeting should take place as soon as possible after participants have been notified, leaving the maximum amount of time remaining for their preparation. The chairman of the program should of course be present if he is not the same person as the one who arranged the meeting. In this way the participants can ask questions of the chairman as to the way he plans to conduct the discussion, and they can confront each other face to face and perhaps contribute suggestions for the manner of carrying out the discussion.

The chairman's outline of the total discussion may or may not be prepared before this planning meeting. If this is prepared, it is helpful to reduce it to one page in length and give each participant a copy. The outline of the total discussion as anticipated by the chairman is particularly helpful to participants in the case of a panel discussion. They can thus see the major areas and ideas to be discussed and the approximate amount of time to be devoted to each. In a radio or television panel, this is a vital consideration and calls for rehearsal of some sort to determine what can be covered in a given amount of time. Participants can also make contributions to add to or revise the suggested outline.

In the case of planning for a symposium or debate, where each speaker is to present a particular solution or point of view, the importance of planning is to insure that the various points of view are all represented and that there is not too much overlapping in the speeches. Sometimes this can be insured by inviting participants from sufficiently different backgrounds. A carpenter, a lawyer, a housewife, and a philosopher may each have different ideas to express about politics or world affairs, so that the chairman could be quite sure they would not all make the same speech. But they might all think exactly alike on a question such as establishing a curfew for teen-agers, and if the chairman wants to be sure that all sides are represented in the discussion, this should be planned in advance.

The planning meeting should also consider the facilities needed for the program. Participants should know whether they are to sit on a raised platform and remain seated for the discussion, as in a panel, or whether there will be a speaker's stand in the center, to which they should come forward and stand while speaking, as in a symposium. They should know in advance whether a public address system will be used. Special considerations such as the presence of guests in the audience or of persons representing particular prejudices should be made known.

6. *Arrange facilities*. For many discussion programs, the group is limited to the use of its regular meeting-room facilities. If this is the case, the person in charge should make every effort to improve these and to have all arrangements made. When he is able to look around and locate the best available facilities for a particular meeting, he should try to meet these suggestions as much as possible.

• The *room* should be bright, cheerful, well-lighted, and large enough to accommodate the total listening group. For some programs, it is preferable to have movable chairs so that their arrangement can be varied. If the total group is small, it is not necessary to have a raised platform for the seating of the participants. This is desirable where the group is large enough to make the problem of seeing the participants difficult for those seated in the rear. It is also helpful to have entrances at both the front and rear of the room so that members coming in late or leaving early can do so with a minimum of disturbance.

• The *arrangement* of tables and chairs must take into account the participating group in the front and the total listening group which may later participate in the forum. If the total group is large and a raised platform is available for the panel, care should be taken to avoid the appearance of a staged program or of setting the panel too much apart from the whole group. The panel should not be seated on a high stage as in a theatre, and if there is a choice between this and seating them on the same floor level with the audience, the latter is preferred.

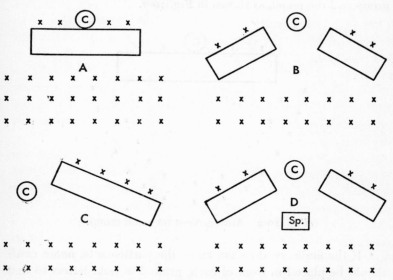

Fig. 10-1   Seating arrangements for discussion programs.

Several basic seating arrangements may be considered, depending on the type of program, and with a number of possible variations. Figure 10-1A represents the typical panel arrangement, with the chairman seated in the center of the participants, all facing the audience directly. Other arrangements for the panel are shown in *B* and *C*, with the latter showing the chairman seated slightly to the side. Any of these arrangements would also be appropriate for the symposium, with *B* being the most typical. In the symposium, the speakers usually stand and come to the center in making their remarks, although in a more informal symposium they may remain at their seats. The arrangement for a debate generally puts the speakers on either side of the platform as shown in diagram *D*, and this arrangement would also be suitable for the symposium. In a debate or symposium where speakers are to come to the center to speak, a speaker's stand should be placed in this position. In a smaller total group, this arrangement will achieve a closer face-to-face relationship among the listening group and the panel, as shown in Fig. 10-2.

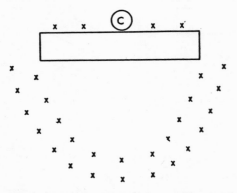

Fig. 10-2   Arrangement for small group.

• If the audience does not know the participants, *name cards* should be placed in front of each, printed in bold letters so that they can be read.

• If necessary to use *microphones* for a public address system, it is of course best to have several placed at proper points on the table in the case of the panel, and one on the speaker's stand if this is to be used in a symposium, debate, or lecture. In the case of any doubt whether a public address system should be used, it is better to eliminate it and have the participants speak up so they can be heard. Particularly in the panel, the public address system adds a mechanical barrier and tends to formalize an otherwise informal and spontaneous discussion. This is especially so when participants have to wait to make their remarks until a microphone is passed around.

• A portable *blackboard* or *chart easel* can add a great deal to the program if it is made available and placed slightly to the right or left behind the chairman. He may wish to record vital facts or figures that should be visualized and kept before the group, as well as main ideas and other points; or individual speakers may wish to use the blackboard or develop charts as they speak. The discussion topic can be written clearly and in full view of the audience before the program starts, in order to stimulate thinking and keep the topic in focus.

7. *Study the subject.* Participants should become as familiar as possible with the subject. If they are already experts and were chosen for this reason, they should need to do little preparing to acquire background information about the subject. Yet any participant would want to get the latest facts and developments, and he would want to select from the material he has the best that will be effective for this particular subject. This might require reading in current periodicals and other literature to find the latest and most timely information. Much of the value of public discussion derives from the attempt to solve problems of a current nature which are making news in the press and magazines.

Preparation in terms of reading on the subject includes the participants, the chairman, and the larger listening group that will later contribute in the forum period. In the case of group discussion in which the entire group participates from the start, everyone should familiarize himself with the subject and come prepared to offer information and opinion based on study and analysis. For the chairman and participants in the program itself, their preparation should include taking notes and accumulating material they will want to bring into the meeting place, perhaps to quote from, to use as handouts, or otherwise to show the audience. All such material and notes should be assembled as the chairman and participants sit down to do their actual preparation in terms of a discussion outline or an outline of their own remarks as participants or speakers.

Here are just a few of the sources of material for information on discussion topics of a current or recent nature:

- *Indexes,* such as *The New York Times Index* and *Reader's Guide to Periodical Literature*
- *Newspapers*
- *Magazines,* such as *Time, Newsweek, Collier's, The Saturday Evening Post, The Atlantic, Harper's Magazine*
- *Reference works,* such as the *World Almanac* and encyclopedias
- *Special publications,* such as "Public Affairs Pamphlets," *Reference Shelf Series, Town Meeting of the Air* pamphlets

Develop a system of recording what you read on cards and keeping them in an alphabetical arrangement. When you refer to a source while speaking, be sure that you are accurate in stating the source and the material itself.

8. *Prepare a discussion outline.* For the chairman of a discussion program, the preparation of the outline for the discussion represents his most specific step in planning a successful event. The outline should include the complete sequence of the discussion from beginning to end, the points to be covered, and questions to be raised. Thorough preparation requires at least two stages. He should first make a detailed outline showing all levels of subpoints and reference material. From this, he might make a more condensed outline which will be the one he will use in conducting the discussion. This should be kept to one page if possible, or two pages at the most. As we pointed out above, it should be reproduced so that a copy can be given to all the panel participants. In the planning meeting with the participants, the chairman can mark on the outline the places where different members will likely contribute. If a symposium is planned, he would indicate the parts of the outline to be covered by each participant in his prepared talk.

The form of the outline should follow the pattern of discussion shown in Chap. 9, and room should be allowed on the left side of the page to indicate special methods or techniques, transitions, time sequence, or other items the chairman feels will be helpful. The outline is to be regarded as a *flexible* guide for the discussion, and both chairman and the participants should be ready to deviate from it as circumstances in the discussion dictate. The following are samples of working outlines from which the chairman would actually conduct a panel or group discussion.

CHAIRMAN'S DISCUSSION OUTLINE

Topic: "How can we solve the problem of racial discrimination in our community?"

30-min panel discussion to be followed by 15–20-min forum period of audience participation.

Panel members: (list names)

INTRODUCTION

	I. Chairman's opening remarks.
	A. Audience greeting.
Attention	B. This subject has recently come into prominent notice in our community.
Importance of question	1. Several incidents.
	2. Newspaper articles and editorials.
	3. Statement by mayor.
Introductions	C. Our panel members come from varied backgrounds to discuss this question.
3 to 5 min	(Introduce members)

Transition MAIN DISCUSSION

Problem	I. What is the problem of racial discrimination in a college community such as ours?
	A. Is it part of a bigger, nationwide problem?
	B. When did the problem start here?
Get facts	C. How is the problem felt here?
	1. Whom does it affect?
12 min	2. In what ways has it been brought to light?
	3. How serious is it?

Setting
standards

15 min

II. What are we aiming for in trying to solve the
problem?
A. Can we eliminate racial prejudice?
B. What other objectives?

Possible
solutions
Get *all*
proposals
before dis-
cussing pros
and cons
of each

III. What are some solutions we should consider?
A. What has been done up to this time?
1.
2.
B. House all students on an equal basis?
C. Provide equal work opportunities?
D. Allow all persons to use town and college
facilities with equal rights?
E. Write letters to newspapers and campus pub-
lications?

The solution

25 min
Action

30 min

IV. Which of these proposals do we feel are best?
A. Let's consider each one.
1. Advantages and values?
2. Disadvantages or new evils?
B. Should we sponsor one particular proposal?
1. Can this be put into action?
2. Who will do it?
3. When will it be done?

Transition

Forum

50 min

FORUM PERIOD AND CONCLUSION

I. What do you folks think of the problem and
our proposals?
A. Do you have more facts on the problem?
B. Do you have other suggestions to solve it?
C. What questions will you raise about the
solutions?

Conclusion

55 min

II. Summary of total discussion.
A. What we have tried to do.
B. Limitations.
C. Our future thinking and action on this ques-
tion.

CHAIRMAN'S DISCUSSION OUTLINE

Topic: "What kind of training in communications should be practiced in industry today?"

30–40-min panel (or group) discussion.

Attention

3 min

I. Opening remarks by chairman.
   A. Importance of subject to this group.
   B. Introduction of panel members, and qualifications.

Problem or *need*

15 min

II. What are the needs for communications in industry?
   A. For what purposes? (inform, draw from employees)
   B. What happens without communication? (dissatisfaction, lack of teamwork, poor morale, rumor)
   C. What is the present lack of communications?
   D. What communication skills are needed? (speaking, conference leading and participating, interviewing, personal relations)

Possible solutions and *standards*

25 min

III. In what ways is training now being conducted to meet these needs?
   A. In what subjects and skills?
   B. What kind of programs?
   C. Who is doing the training?
   D. What outstanding examples and methods are there?

Solution

35 min

IV. What training programs should be conducted?
   A. What are the most essential subjects and skills?
   B. Who should do the training?
   C. Who should take the training?
   D. What length and kind of programs?
   E. Where should they be conducted?

Action

40 min

V. Do we want to recommend specific action at this time?
   A. Who will carry it out?
   B. What are the details?

VI. Questions and discussion from audience (if a forum period is to follow panel discussion).

VII. Summary and closing remarks by chairman.

199

In the second outline, the parenthetical items are the possible answers to the questions as the chairman would like to have them brought out. It is frequently helpful to insert some of these in the outline, so that occasional leading questions may be raised which will induce the desired points from the participants. This is particularly true in an informational or instructional discussion, where the chairman feels some responsibility for insuring that certain information come before the group.

9. *Prepare a speech outline (or other notes as a participant).* We have already emphasized the importance of preparation for discussion by participants as well as leaders or chairmen. Practically all the points we have suggested above are applicable to the participant in looking forward to his part in the discussion program. He is primarily responsible for his own participation, but he also owes a responsibility to the chairman and the group as a whole to see that the program is successful. He will want to know the nature and purpose of the meeting, the type of discussion, the exact wording of the topic, the other participants, the physical setting and facilities available, as much as he can about the subject, and the part he plays in the total discussion in relation to the others.

If the program is a *panel* discussion, he will not prepare any formal speech. He should prepare along the following lines:

- Assess his present knowledge and ideas on the subject
- Determine to what extent he should obtain more information
- Study and reflect on the chairman's outline and his own analysis of the questions to be taken up, to determine at what points he feels he will most likely want to contribute to the discussion
- Locate the areas or issues where he is apt to be in disagreement with other panel members
- List the points or questions he would like to raise for others to discuss, in the absence of the chairman covering these points

Any member of the larger listening group, or of a group planning to hold a *group discussion* without a preliminary program, should go through similar steps in preparing for his part in the meeting.

An individual participant preparing for a *symposium* or *debate* (or a single prepared speech) should prepare for the speech by making an outline of his own remarks, after he has gone through the above steps. In this role, he is making a speech as an individual, but he is also a member of a discussion group. His speech, therefore, should not be given as though in a void without his considering what others have said and will say; it should be adapted to the remarks of others. This should show in the introduction as well as in the handling of points during his speech, and in the conclusion. Otherwise, his outline is very much the same as any speech outline.

Assuming a symposium program on the same subject as our outline above on racial discrimination, your part as third speaker is to handle the point dealing with student housing and your suggestions for this. Your outline might look something like this:

OUTLINE FOR SYMPOSIUM PARTICIPANT

Topic: "How can we solve the problem of racial discrimination in our community?"

My speech purpose: To discuss my suggestions for solving the problem of student housing as it relates to racial discrimination.

Length: 7 to 8 min

INTRODUCTION

First
speaker

I. Adaptation to first two speakers

    A. First speaker has analyzed the problem. I should like to add these brief facts to what he has said.

        1.

        2.

Second
speaker

    B. The second speaker's review of the many possible solutions is most interesting and challenging.

1. It might be well if we could adopt them all.
2. I should like to talk further about one, dealing with housing.

Transition

MAIN DISCUSSION

Review of problem

I. There are many evidences of racial discrimination in student housing today.
   A. On the campus.
      1. Examples.
      2. Statement by Dean of Men.
   B. In the community.
      1.
      2.

Proposed solution

II. I would propose that all campus housing facilities be opened to minority groups.
   A. Dormitories.
   B. Fraternities and sororities.
   C. Other.

III. We have already adopted this policy for dormitories.
   A. Present policy explained.
   B. Many other universities have this policy.
      1.
      2.

Proof of proposals

IV. Doing this in sororities and fraternities and other groups is more difficult.
   A. They are mostly national organizations.
   B. Some organizations have adopted this policy.
      1.
      2.
   C. There is considerable evidence around the country.

V. We have much less control over the community housing facilities.

      A. We can try to influence them, however, by doing these things:
        1.
        2.
      B. This will require concerted effort.

CONCLUSION

Summary
     I. I hope we can all give further thought to these suggestions.
      A.
      B.
      C.

Adaptation
     II. It will be interesting to see whether all of you feel we can do these things.

10. *Consider what publicity is needed.* This may or may not be a necessary step. In an organization meeting regularly, the program for the next meeting can always be announced at the previous meeting, and this may be sufficient notice. But even under such conditions, it is well to follow this with a postcard or letter announcement to the members. If the program is open to the public, the extent to which publicity is needed has to be determined in each case. Such factors as the importance of the subject and participants, the facilities available, and time may influence the publicity. The program chairman should consider the outlets at his disposal, including newspaper stories, posters, radio announcements, letters, telephone calls, and others, in planning just what would be most effective in the particular situation. In planning for more important events, printed programs might be made to give to all those attending.

Participants who take the time to prepare are usually pleased to see a public announcement of the program. If appropriate, a story about the discussion may be sent to newspapers after it is over.

Conclusion

The responsibility for carrying out a successful discussion program starts in the early planning stages and involves going through a series of steps to insure complete preparation. Although some of the steps may be handled rather quickly, none of them should be skipped. In order to be sure that you include them all, use this check list.

DISCUSSION PROGRAM PLANNING CHECK LIST

1. Have I determined the nature of the MEETING and GROUP?   _____
2. Has the best TYPE OF DISCUSSION been selected?   _____
3. Is the TOPIC a good one?
   • Will it interest the maximum number?   _____
   • Is it properly worded?   _____
4. What about the PARTICIPANTS?   _____
   • Selected with all factors considered?   _____
   • Notified as to topic and responsibilities?   _____
   • Understand type of meeting? Program?   _____
5. Is a PLANNING MEETING to be held?   _____
   • Everyone notified?   _____
   • All items considered?   _____
6. Have FACILITIES been arranged?   _____
   • Room engaged?   _____
   • Tables and chairs arranged?   _____
   • Name cards, blackboard, speaker's stand?   _____
7. Have I fully studied the SUBJECT?   _____
   • Any special references to look at?   _____
   • Items to bring to the program?   _____
8. Have I prepared a DISCUSSION OUTLINE?   _____
   • Considered the total discussion?   _____
   • Given each participant a copy?   _____
   • Explained each participant's part?   _____
9. Have I prepared as a PARTICIPANT?   _____
10. Is PUBLICITY properly provided for?   _____

APPLYING THIS CHAPTER

1. Choose several topics of current interest and phrase them as good questions for discussion programs. Phrase the same topics as debate questions.
2. Using one of these topics, make an outline of how you would lead a panel discussion.
3. How might you divide one of the topics for a good symposium program?
4. What was wrong with the arrangements at a discussion meeting you attended recently? Could these have been improved with better planning?
5. Where might you best look for information on a particular subject on which you will participate in a discussion program?
6. What is the value of calling a panel together in advance of the program to go over the outline? Are there some disadvantages?

CHAPTER 11

Leadership and Participation in Discussion Programs

WE ARE NOW ready to apply the concepts and principles of leadership and participation to the various types of public discussion programs and meetings.[1] The leader or participant, with a clear understanding of the distinguishing characteristics of his program and with a feeling that his preparation is complete, now turns his attention to the techniques and methods he will employ in the actual discussion. In this chapter we will point these up specifically for each type of program, after we have first looked at the role of the chairman and the participant in public discussion.

The Role of the Chairman

The leader of a panel, symposium, or debate is usually referred to as the "chairman," with this label also frequently applied to the presiding officer of a business meeting and in other group

---

[1] Most of the discussion of Leadership and Participation in Chaps. 6 and 7 is applicable to the public discussion chairman and participant, and the concepts and principles suggested in those chapters should be applied.

discussion situations. He is also referred to as the "discussion leader" and as "moderator." In a sense he occupies a dual role, or perhaps we should say his role has two parts: he is chairman of the smaller discussion group up front, and he is then chairman (or leader of the discussion) for the entire group.

The discussion chairman may or may not be the person in charge of the meeting as a whole. In the case of a discussion program as part of a regular meeting of an organization, the presiding officer of the meeting may introduce the discussion program chairman, who then proceeds with the program. After it is finished, he will probably turn the chairmanship back to the presiding officer, who will adjourn the meeting.

The chairman's role is always that of impartial leader of the discussion. He should never take sides or indicate his own position or points of view. He should never make comments on remarks or speeches of the participants that would indicate or even imply his own agreement, disagreement, approval, or disapproval of what has been said. His primary role is to guide and stimulate the discussion through a planned sequence. In doing this, he exercises little or no control over what is said, and such control that he does exercise is in regard to calling on and recognizing speakers and to keeping some organized pattern to the discussion. The way in which he does this varies considerably, according to different types of programs, as we shall see below.

The Role of the Participant

The participant in a public discussion program is both an individual and a part of a group, though he probably has more concern for his place in the group as a whole than he would have if he were in a private discussion situation such as a conference. In other words, he is less free to speak his own mind fully, partly because of the public nature of the program and partly because there is apt to be more planning as to the part he is supposed to play. This does not necessarily mean that the average discussion program is more structured than the average conference, for the participants are normally quite free to express their own points of view and the outcome is rarely predictable in advance. But if the discussion chairman has carried out his planning and preparation steps and has met with the participants, they should feel more inclined to regard the program as a group effort. This may also be the feeling of most participants in conferences, but it is a feeling that is usually harder to develop in the conference situation.

The participant's attitude should be one of open-mindedness, objectivity, and conciliation, all of which should add up to a *cooperative attitude.* In this sense, he *inquires* and *reflects,* rather than advocates. Yet his remarks are made out of conviction and are frequently persuasive when he is offering opinion and judgment. His participation is rather interesting to analyze in this respect, for persuasive speaking is not entirely consistent with reflection and inquiry. The inconsistency is more apparent than real, however, if one looks at the participant's total role. While maintaining an over-all attitude of inquiry and open-mindedness, he can still persuade and argue for his own position as he makes his remarks and relates them to the total remarks of others. But as others contribute their opinions, which might differ from his, he is free to modify his own and even to accept theirs as he practices cooperation and joins in the total *group effort* toward the best solution. The spirit of true cooperative discussion, therefore, should move him in the direction of submerging his own will to that of the group.

The question of the relationship between the small participating group and the total listening group also poses a dual role for the individual. He is initially a member of the small program group, and the exchange of ideas is primarily among the members of that group. The participant is thus communicating with the others around the table, and his remarks should be directed to them, both in thought and in actual physical communication. Assuming A, B, C, and D around a table, when A speaks, he looks at one or all of B, C, and D. His larger listening audience hears this communication, and A is also speaking it to them, but he must choose between them and the panel members for his primary source of communicativeness. He should regard his participation as being with and among the panel, but he should always be aware of the larger group, speak loud enough for them to hear him, and occasionally direct a remark toward them by looking in their direction.

The participant's manner of speaking should be adapted to the group situation. When he speaks from the front of the room, he should be sure that he is heard by all. The most common pitfall in this respect is to fail to *project* the voice so that all in the room can hear him. This is partly a matter of speaking loudly enough, but it also includes keeping the head up, opening the mouth, and letting the voice come out. And projection is not enhanced by leaning on an elbow, keeping the hand over the mouth while resting the chin in it, burying the head in notes on the table, or slouching or reclining in the chair. These pitfalls not only result in poor projection, but they are a giveaway of an uninterested, apathetic attitude which will do anything but gain respect for your remarks from either the immediate group or the listening group.

Most informal discussion is from a seated position. This makes communication and projection even more difficult to achieve. In a symposium, debate, or lecture, the speaker is standing, probably at a speaker's stand, and should observe all the rules of good speech delivery. When you are speaking as a member of a larger group from the floor, it is well to consider the advisability of standing in the given case, particularly if the group is large or if the custom of others is to stand.

The use of notes by the participant should also be considered in regard to the particular situation. In making informal and spontaneous remarks, notes would probably be very much in the way, but there is no harm in having them at your place on the table and occasionally glancing at them for reference. In making a more formal presentation, notes may be used by putting them neatly on small cards, familiarizing yourself with them so that a quick glance is sufficient, and not allowing them to interfere with you and your listener. Let us now observe some more specific techniques of participation in various types of situations.

Leadership and Participation in Various Types of Programs

We will now attempt to describe the adaptation of leadership and participation principles and methods to the various types of discussion programs.

THE PANEL

Special Features

In the panel, participants are seated at a table in the front of the room facing the larger audience, usually with the chairman in the center. Both participants and chairman remain seated during the panel discussion. The exchange is informal, spontaneous, and often impromptu, yet the discussion should follow a pattern of organization that has been prepared in advance. The panel is the most informal of all the types of planned discussion programs, resembling the small conference or committee discussion.

Leadership

The chairman of a panel discussion resembles very much the conference leader in a private conference room, except that both he and the participants are conscious of the larger listening group at all times. His tools and methods of leadership are very similar to those used in the conference, so that most of what we said about leadership in Chap. 6 would apply.

There are some misconceptions about the chairman's responsibilities in relation to those of the participants. The first of these is the belief that the success of the program depends only on the chairman. We of course know that all participants share the chairman's responsibility for keeping the discussion on the track. The fact that panel members do not make speeches also gives rise to the misconception that preparation is not required. We have already pointed out that because of the extreme flexibility of the panel, knowledge of all phases of the subject is probably more important to both chairman and participants than when they are making a prepared speech. The third and perhaps most fatal misconception is the notion that participants should sit back and wait for the chairman to call on them before making remarks. When every contribution must be solicited by the chairman, who then comments after each, there is a formal and stilted atmosphere which makes for a slow and uninteresting discussion. Members should be alert to break in spontaneously and offer comments without waiting for the chairman to call on them.

Here are some of the specific things a chairman should do:

1. Open by introducing the topic and its timeliness, and introducing the panel members. It is usually not necessary to stand to do this, unless the listening group is quite large. The participants should not stand when they are thus introduced.

2. Get the discussion started by posing a question, preferably a general or overhead question rather than one directed to a specific participant. If the discussion can start with a voluntary series of remarks, it is apt to remain that way rather than develop into a formal series of questions, remarks, and comment in turn between the chairman and each member.

3. Keep the discussion organized, following a flexible outline which is familiar to the participants before the discussion. The chairman can make notations on his outline of the names of participants who are most likely to contribute on different points, or those he can call on by direct question, if this is necessary.

4. Guide and stimulate the discussion among *all* the participants. An effort should be made to get silent members to talk by raising specific questions and by pointing up the discussion in ways that will stimulate their interest. Direct questions should be avoided unless it is quite certain that the individual asked the question will respond.

5. Use more general or overhead questions than direct questions. The general question will stimulate *total* group interest. It

should be followed up, however, with narrower and more analytical questions if this is not successful.

6. Encourage free, open, and informal participation. This can be done by maintaining an impartial position, refraining from participation as a member while acting as chairman, using appropriate humor, and being a *good listener*.

7. Resolve tension and argument by tact and humor, and by preventing heated exchange and argument from developing between two persons.

8. Make occasional transitions and internal summaries to keep the organization of the discussion clearly before the members. When sufficient time has been devoted to one point, the chairman should indicate that the group is going on to the next point and should summarize what has been discussed to date. The group should always know clearly what point is before it.

9. Watch the time so that the program starts and ends promptly. The chairman should also keep note of the time as the discussion proceeds in order to insure that all points are discussed. In the case of a participant's talking too long, he should tactfully break in (at the end of a sentence) and turn the discussion to another participant or to another point.

10. Use the blackboard, charts, or other visual aids to enhance the discussion when appropriate. He will usually have to stand to do this, in which case he should return to his seat and proceed with the discussion after the point has been made.

11. Summarize the discussion and make a proper transition to the forum period in which the larger audience will participate. This summary should not be lengthy, nor should it attempt to restate everything that has been covered. It is more a brief statement of review and is more important as a transition for the start of the forum period.

12. Be *group-centered* rather than self-centered at all times.

Participation

We have already commented on some of the misconceptions about both leadership and participation in a panel discussion, and we have pointed out some suggestions for the role of the participant. Putting these together and applying them to the particular role of membership in a panel, here are some of the specific things a participant should do:

1. Feel that he is thoroughly prepared by reading on the subject, analyzing the chairman's and his own outline, and anticipating where he might make the most valuable contributions.

2. Be group-centered rather than self-centered in his attitude toward the discussion topic and in his relations with other members of the group. He should remember that the panel is a co-operative effort and be willing to submerge his own feelings and interests to those of the group.

3. Help the chairman keep the discussion organized and within approximate time limits. If the chairman fails to exercise his own duties and responsibilities as a chairman, or if he needs help, an individual participant may assume certain of these duties. He should not do these things, however, if the chairman is doing them.

4. *Break in and contribute spontaneously without waiting to be called on by the chairman.* This is probably the most important suggestion for participants in order to insure a real panel discussion, which should be informal and conversational. The participant should be ready to *offer* comment at the very start of the discussion, and from then on he should be an *active* participant, not a passive one. Good participation requires a lively, animated physical and mental attitude. In breaking in spontaneously, he should not interrupt a speaker, yet he must be extremely alert to come in with his contribution at a strategic time. If he waits until the speaker is completely finished and pauses, another participant may already start to speak. The timing of a remark is important, and its purpose may be lost after the passage of time and after several others have spoken.

5. Make no long speeches, but rather make brief remarks more often. Any individual remark in a discussion should not run over a minute or so in length. If you have more to say than this, it is better to say it in a series of several remarks. This is particularly true when you have several points to make. Make just one point at a time, rather than trying to cover too much in one contribution. No one likes the long-winded or the chain speaker who goes on at length from one point to another, each one reminding him of something else.

6. *Be a good listener.* If our previous point about breaking in spontaneously was our most important suggestion, this one runs a close second. Participation means listening as well as speaking. And it means being an active listener, always attentive and sympathetic and equally interested in the remarks of *all other* participants.

7. Talk loudly enough to be heard by everyone in the listening audience.

8. Speak primarily to other panel members, and occasionally in the direction of the larger audience.

9. Be open-minded and conciliatory rather than dogmatic. Feel free to take issue with the points of view of others, but do this pleasantly and tactfully, and use the principles of conciliation rather than argument, as we discussed them in Chap. 7. The participant should express himself out of the feelings and convictions he has, yet he should be ready to adapt these to the points of other speakers and try to recognize the values of their opinions as well as his own.

10. Sometimes use the occasion of answering a point to make a transition and introduce a new point you want to bring into the discussion. By doing this, you can divert attention away from argument and into another area of interest.

THE SYMPOSIUM

Special Features

While the panel resembles most closely the informal give-and-take of a face-to-face conference, the symposium resembles more the public speaking situation of a series of speeches to an audience. However, it would be a mistake to regard it as a series of isolated speeches, for what makes the symposium a type of discussion is the fact that all the speeches are integrated and aimed toward a common goal, usually of solving a problem. This is a *group goal,* just as is the panel, and each participant should speak as a member of the group as well as an individual speaker.

The symposium speakers may be seated at one table facing the audience, as in the panel, though frequently they are at two separate tables, with a speaker's stand in the front center.

Leadership

The symposium chairman is largely an introducer of speakers during the formal part of the program. But he too must keep in mind the integrated nature of the remarks and do all he can to help bring the thoughts of the speakers closer together as the program unfolds. After the speeches are finished, he may carry on a brief informal exchange among the participants before starting the forum period with the larger audience. This very much resembles the panel discussion.

Here are some suggestions for the symposium chairman:

1. Open the session with appropriate greetings and introduction of the topic, pointing up its timeliness. Then introduce the participants, usually by starting at one end of the table and going around the group. Or they may be introduced in the order of speaking. Introductions should give a brief indication of the background of the speaker to point up particularly his qualifications to speak on the subject. In most instances, all the speakers will be introduced before the first speaker is presented, though some chairmen prefer to wait and introduce each person as he is called on to talk. All introductions should be comparatively brief, so that the chairman's total time would not be over three to five minutes. He should stand while making introductions and transition remarks between speeches.

2. After each speech, the chairman should make some brief comment on what has been said (although never to indicate approval or disapproval, or agreement or disagreement), with appropriate transition remarks in presenting the next speaker. Depending on how this has been worked out in advance with the participants, he may simply say, "John Brown will be our next speaker," or he may indicate that "John Brown will now tell us what he thinks of Mr. Smith's proposal and will present his solution." The latter reveals more clearly to the audience how the discussion is unfolding and the integration of the speeches.

3. Have some system for timing the speeches and for giving a warning signal to the speakers when their time is up. This is one of the more difficult problems in keeping a symposium on the track according to plan, for speakers will usually want to speak longer than the time allotted to them.

4. Resolve conflict by humor or tactful remark if the argument between any two speakers gets too intense.
5. Listen carefully to all speakers so that he has their remarks well in mind during the discussion and forum period.
6. Assist the speakers in using the blackboard, charts, or other visual aids in presenting their talks.
7. Make brief summary remarks when the speeches are finished. At this point, a brief informal panel discussion may be held among the participants, depending on how the program has been arranged. Even if this is not planned, the chairman should be alert to determine whether this is desirable in situations where one speaker may want to reply briefly to the remarks of another before starting the forum period.
8. Make a transition to the forum period, after which closing remarks should be made, including thanking the speakers.

Participation

The chief nature of the symposium speaker's participation is the presentation of his talk in the program. However, he must also be prepared to comment on all phases of the topic and on issues which are not necessarily covered in his formal speech. Specifically, he should:

1. Come to the speaker's stand (or center) to present his talk.[2] This should be communicated primarily to the larger listening audience, with an occasional indication that he is also talking to his colleagues on the platform by turning to them or the chairman. He may use notes if he does not allow them to get in the way of good direct speaking.
2. Open his talk with some reference and adaptation to other speakers' remarks. If he is the first speaker, this adaptation would be directed toward the chairman, the topic, and the listening audience, to achieve common ground. Following speakers should leave about one-fourth of their total speaking time for introductory handling of points of preceding speakers. This can be in the nature of adding information and supplementing what has been said, or of expressing agreement or disagreement. Words such as "disagree" should be avoided in favor of indicating one's position

[2] In a very informal symposium, participants may remain seated, so that it resembles a panel.

less dogmatically, always being careful to give some credit to the point being refuted.

3. Move into the main points of his own prepared remarks by making proper transition from his introduction and indicating clearly what points he is to take up. This does not mean that he cannot use an indirect method for getting into his points, but the speaker should not make it too difficult for the audience to follow him.

4. Use good reasoning and factual supporting material to develop his points. Make use of examples, analogies, illustrations such as stories, data, and statistics, and statements of authority. Be concrete and specific in order best to hold listener attention and interest.

5. Stay within the time limit. Any participant who goes beyond the time allotted to him to any extent is infringing on the time of the other speakers or the audience as a whole in the forum period.

6. Listen to the remarks of all the other participants, both better to integrate them with his own speech and better to participate in the forum period. The integration of others' points within one's own prepared remarks is an ability everyone strives for as a good discussion participant. The good speaker who can do this throughout his speech need not necessarily set aside a specific time for adaptation only in his introduction.

THE DEBATE

Special Features

We have already observed in Chap. 9 that debate is not typically discussion, in that the debater has a fixed position and point of view to uphold and will not allow the discussion to influence this. We have also pointed out that the debate process is an integral part of the total discussion process in that it takes place during the phase of discussion where the best solution and action to be taken are sought by the group. Our interest here, however, is to point out the distinguishing features of leadership and participation in debate as a formal discussion program presented before a larger group. Since the debate program resembles the symposium in many ways, we can include most of the suggestions made above for the debate chairman and the participants.

Leadership

The debate chairman usually sits in the center of the platform, flanked on either side by the affirmative and negative speakers sitting at separate tables. His introduction of the topic and speakers is very similar to the symposium, with the sequence alternating from affirmative to negative. He should be standing in making all introductions and transition remarks.

Participation

We are not attempting here to treat all the principles and techniques of formal debate as they would be studied and practiced by a member of a university debate society. The chief distinguishing feature of participation in debate, which we have already mentioned for the symposium but which is even more important in debate, is the factor of careful analysis of issues and logical reasoning and thinking. Debate is a true challenge to thinking and reasoning ability, for one's opponents are alert to find flaws and to uncover weaknesses in reasoning or evidence. These points of debate participation should be emphasized:

1. One's attitude in debate should be properly adjusted in relation to the subject, the opponents, and the listening audience. Although he steadfastly sticks to the position he prepared to defend, the debater must have a healthy regard for the other side of the proposition and for his opponents' right to uphold that side. He must also respect them as individuals and never attack them as persons. Argument should be directed toward the issues, *never toward the man.* A proper attitude includes keeping one's perspective, temper, and sense of humor. It includes maintaining a pleasant relationship with all participants and the handling of refutation and rebuttal in a way that recognizes this relationship, as pointed out in earlier chapters.

2. Refutation, or the answering of opponents' arguments, should be woven throughout the main speeches in a debate. *Rebuttal* is the answering of arguments during the final rebuttal speeches, which are devoted almost entirely to this, in addition to a summary. The early part of one's main speech should be devoted to adapta-

tion and refutation. The good debater also weaves refutation throughout his speech, showing where his own constructive points are answers to points made by his opponents. There are a number of ways of answering an argument that you want to refute, including:

a. Pointing out that it is not relevant or important to the question.

b. Showing that it is not supported by the facts, or that insufficient evidence has been given.

c. Indicating fallacies in reasoning.

d. Arriving at a contrary argument by sound reasoning.

e. Supplying more and better evidence to support your side of the argument.

f. Confessing the argument but showing that it does not help the opponent's side.

g. Turning the argument so that it actually helps your side.

In the rebuttal, each point taken up should be stated clearly and handled, then a clear transition should be made to the next point. First rebuttal speakers should handle as many points of opponents as time will allow, being sure to include the important points. Final rebuttal speakers should spend a major amount of their time making a summary and a "balance" of the two sides, in which they make their own side stand out as better.

3. Make each point and the presentation of the entire side you are representing consistent with points made by your colleague, who is also upholding your side. Debaters should not be caught in inconsistencies. This requires careful planning and preparation of your *case*, which is the sum total of points to be made on your side. The outline of the total case is to be made in detail and is called a *brief*. The brief should show all the main points and subpoints and the evidence to be used by each speaker.

4. In answering points of the other side, it is well to have a large supply of evidence you can draw on to support your position. The introduction of new evidence added to what has already been presented is of greater value than repeating or rephrasing evidence already used.

5. A knowledge of the attitude of the audience (as well as the information they have) on the question will be helpful in determining whether the listening group is favorably or unfavorably disposed to what you are saying. This will also be helpful in anticipating questions that will be raised during the forum period.

6. A card-index file should be kept of all points and evidence that might be used, with some system worked out so that you or your colleague can quickly draw on the material you want to include at any given stage in the debate. It is best to reduce all evidence to cards that can be kept neatly in one place rather than to approach the speaker's stand with a variety of newspapers, magazines, clippings, and books.

THE LECTURE

The lecture comes within the scope of our consideration of leading and participating in various discussion situations only in the sense that it is followed by a forum period wherein the total group participates. The chairman's job is to introduce the speaker, pointing up his background and qualifications, his particular interest in this subject, any special relationship with the audience, and the importance of the subject. After doing this, and before the speaker is presented, the chairman should also explain to the audience the nature of the discussion period that will follow the lecture. When the speaker is finished, he usually goes back to his seat while the chairman again comes forward and makes appropriate transition remarks regarding the forum period. At this time, he should indicate to the audience whether they should address their questions directly to the speaker or through the chairman, or any other details for handling the discussion with the speaker.

If a lecture-forum is planned, the speaker's talk should be timed so that at least one-third of the total time of the meeting is left for the participation by the audience. Depending on whether the speaker's purpose is to supply information or knowledge as in a learning situation, or to present a point of view on a controversial topic, questions from the group may seek further information or indicate controversial areas on which they want further comment. Both the speaker's participation and the chairman's duties in the forum period are discussed below.

THE FORUM

We have already defined a forum as that part of a total discussion situation where the entire membership of the group participates, usually after a discussion program has been presented by a few persons (or just one, as in the lecture). All of the above programs are usually followed by a forum period, and it is run quite the same in each, except for the number of persons who might be participating and the degree of formality in each case. Although a forum involves the participation of everyone in the room, it differs from group discussion as such in that the questions and comments tend to be directed vertically from the front toward the listening group and back, with little horizontal or cross participation among the members of the larger group itself. *Yet every comment made in a forum period is for the benefit of everyone in the room, not just the person asking a question and the participant who is answering it.* Many of the suggestions made for the leader and the participants are in order to further this fundamental objective.

Forum Leadership

The chairman of the panel, symposium, debate, or other type of discussion program now becomes the leader of the group participation. His job is to see that the maximum amount of discussion takes place in the time available, with the largest possible number of persons participating. To do this he must stimulate, spread, and guide the discussion and sometimes serve as interpreter or moderator if disputes or misunderstandings arise. Here are some suggestions:

1. The transition from the planned program of the smaller group to the start of the forum period for the entire membership is often difficult. Sometimes several persons are eager to raise questions or make comments, but frequently everyone holds back for someone else to start. Once the discussion is started, it usually

snowballs, so that the problem of the leader is one of controlling and spreading it properly. But he must be prepared to prime the start of the discussion by having ready some pointed questions which he might raise in his remarks to the larger group to stimulate their thinking, or to direct a question himself at the panel in general or to a specific panel member, or to call on someone in the larger group who he is quite sure will respond. Some suggest that a question should actually be planted in the audience in order to insure that the question period gets off to a good start.

2. The procedure in asking questions or making comments from the group should be explained by the forum leader. Usually it is suggested that questions be directed to the panel in general, or to a specific member of the panel. The leader should indicate whether he will receive the questions and pass them on to the panel members for answer, or whether they will receive them. The size of the group and the degree of informality will frequently dictate the method used. In a small group situation, the leader tends to retreat into the background while the questions are asked directly of the speakers, and he comes forward to make transitions and interpretations and to help stimulate or spread the participation. He must be sure that everyone hears and understands the question. If the group and room are large, *it is best that he repeat the question so that all can hear it* and then turn it over to the proper participant for reply. If the leader does not do this and the participant receives the question directly from the group member, he should restate it before he answers it if there is any doubt as to whether the total group heard and understood it.

3. The leader should not allow one person to speak at length from the floor or to insist on asking a series of questions. This sometimes occurs when a question is put to a speaker who answers it and the questioner is either dissatisfied with the answer or wants to continue cross-examining the speaker. A little of this may add interest, but such an individual soon is taking up the time of others who want the floor. The leader should tactfully interrupt and point this out while recognizing the next questioner.

4. The time factor must be kept in mind during the forum period, so that the maximum spread of discussion is achieved. As many as possible should be recognized for comment or questions. Answering questions should also be spread among the participants in

the original program. Frequently, one or two persons are singled out by the audience for most of their questions. If this is what the group wishes, it is hard for the chairman to interrupt, but he should step in and suggest that questions might be put to other members of the panel. Or he may draw in silent members by posing direct questions to them.

5. The position of the leader during the forum period may vary, depending on the physical arrangement and the degree of formality. If the original program was a panel, he might remain seated throughout the forum, along with the participants. Usually he will stand to open the forum and remain standing, then retreat to a side position so that the person answering the question may have the center position. He should then come to the center for receiving questions or for making comments or transitions, or for calling on a participant, then move again to the side. The main objective is to give the center of attention to the individual speaking or answering a question.

6. After the time for the forum period has elapsed, the leader should make brief summary remarks, thank the speakers, and either adjourn the meeting or turn it back to the presiding officer for adjournment. It is better to stop a discussion while members still want to participate rather than let it die out.

In a large and more formal setting, it is sometimes requested that questions be written out and handed to the chairman before they are accepted. This method should be used only when necessary, for it makes the forum period stilted and less interesting and takes away from the members of the group the opportunity to get up on their feet and participate. The whole group feels the question as coming from them when it is spoken rather than presented in writing.

The *buzz session* is another method for getting the group to feel more involved in the total discussion period and to feel that each question belongs to everyone. It is most useful in rather large groups, particularly following a lecture, in order to give everyone an opportunity to discuss the speaker's points. The procedure for the buzz session, sometimes called the Phillips 66 for its founder, J. Donald Phillips, is to divide the large group into small groups of twelve (the number and seating arrangement may be varied), who face each other in a six-and-six arrangement to talk over what they have heard. This discussion is to last for a given period announced by the chairman, after which the groups each choose a representative who will present one question or comment which the group decided they wanted to put to the speaker during the forum period. This method is said by its proponents to foster a feeling of greater involvement among the members and to have the advantages of insuring participation by all and providing a systematic coverage of the entire group during the forum period. When used for these purposes, it is a worthwhile technique. There is some tendency to overdo its use, however, and to regard it as a panacea for all forum discussion. It should not be used where the total group is small enough to allow for a good spread of participation. It has a tendency to formalize the forum period in that everyone knows that these and only these questions will be asked and so some will sit back and lose interest, for there is a lack of the spontaneity which comes when no one is sure where the next question is coming from. The time spent in organizing the buzz-session groups may often be spent to better advantage in general discussion, particularly when the size does not warrant the use of this method.

Forum Participation

We are concerned with participation in the forum by both members of the larger group and members of the discussion program which preceded the forum.

• *By group members.* All the members of the listening group should feel a responsibility to contribute during the forum period. Actually, they should be appreciative of the opportunity to question and take issue with the speakers as one of the prized values of the democratic process. Even though everyone in the room cannot be given a chance to speak, because of problems of time and group size, they should all seek the opportunity and help in stimulating the total group participation. Specifically, these suggestions are in order:

1. One should be recognized by the chairman before he takes the floor and starts to speak. Usually raising a hand is the way to gain recognition. If he is not recognized or does not get his opportunity during the entire period, the group member should accept this as the way democracy operates and should still be an active listener to the remarks of others.

2. Participation from the floor is generally confined to questions, rather than lengthy comment, although some comment and expression of opinion is in order unless the chairman has explained otherwise. The participant should stand and speak loudly enough to be heard by all in the room, and he should direct his question as advised by the chairman.

3. Questions should be brief and carefully worded. After a question is answered, perhaps one follow-up question is in order, but only under unusual circumstances should a questioner feel he has the right to continue an unlimited stream of questions.

4. One should always be conscious of his obligations in regard to the other group members who want to contribute. He should also refrain from directing remarks across the floor to other group members unless a period of general group discussion has been indicated by the chairman.

• *By program participants.* The chief responsibility of the panel (debate, symposium, or lecture) speaker during the forum is to be an alert listener at all times and to answer questions put to him by the group member or by the chairman. In doing this, he should:

1. Usually come forward to the center, unless an informal panel is followed by an informal forum period in a comparatively small group. He should speak loudly enough to be heard throughout the room. He should direct his answer or remarks toward the person asking the question but should not assume that his answer is only for the questioner's benefit. The stimulation of all group members from both the questions and the answers is one of the chief values of the forum period.

2. He should restate the question clearly before answering it. Then

he might make some comment indicating that he is pleased by the question or that it is appropriate. Even though the question implies disagreement with what he has said, he should indicate that he welcomes this and gives credit to the questioner. Tact and diplomacy are essential in doing this. He should analyze the question to determine whether more information or explanation is sought or whether an opinion or point of view is requested.

3. In answering the question, he should state his main point or opinion in regard to it clearly, then follow this up with fact or other supporting material. The answer should be comparatively brief. If it takes more than two minutes, the answer turns into a speech. The speaker should be careful that he does not get involved in lengthy remarks in the forum period or that he does not get into a chain of points that occur to him one after another while he is answering a question.

4. No one speaker on the platform should want to usurp too much of the forum time. He should encourage remarks from his panel members and give way to one of them who might want to comment on the same point he is answering. Likewise, every speaker should be alert while others are answering questions and seek recognition by the chairman to add his thoughts to those of the persons speaking.

5. Careful listening by every participant is essential in order to be able to carry out all these suggestions.

THE FILM-FORUM

Films have become an established medium for stimulating interest prior to the general discussion of a topic by a group. The 16mm sound motion picture and the 35mm filmstrip with sound are the most common types of films used for this purpose. The basic purpose of the film, when it is to be followed by a forum period, is to set a background for the discussion that is to follow, or to provide instruction in the case of a learning situation. The chairman of such a program should keep these things in mind:

1. Arrange the physical facilities so that everyone is in good view of the screen and not too close to the projector. See that the audio speaker is in the best possible position for all to hear.

2. Preview the film so that you have a thorough understanding of its length and the points it brings out. Make a list of these points either to hand out to the group members or to use as a basis for carrying on the discussion.

3. Prepare for starting the forum discussion period by having in mind what questions you want the group to consider first. It is best to talk about the over-all purpose and message of the film, then take it up point by point.

4. Give everyone an opportunity to ask questions and to clarify items brought out in the film.

5. Before showing the film, point out to the group why it is being shown and ask them to look for certain things in the film. This will make their listening more attentive and will afford a basis for discussion of these same points in the forum period.

6. Use the blackboard or chart easel for putting before the group the main ideas they should get from the film. Sometimes this is valuable to do before the showing, although it can be done to advantage during the forum period as the points are raised by the group.

7. Do not continue the discussion after it is apparent that there are no further questions and that the group understands the points of the film.

8. Summarize what has been gained from the program.

There are many **sources for obtaining films,** including college and university and government agency film libraries, commercial distributors and producers, and others. Some of the major compilations listing films and sources of rental and purchase are given in the Visual Aids section on p. 253 of this book.

GROUP DISCUSSION

It is fitting that we tie together some thoughts on group discussion as the final subject heading in this book, for we referred to it in an earlier chapter as the label frequently applied to the process of discussion in all group situations. All the pages of this analysis of the various types of discussion situations and the plans, methods, and principles for carrying them out add up to the total of discussion techniques. If the reader applies the principles and suggestions in the given situation which best suit that situation, he will be able to lead or participate in any kind of discussion.

If there is any particular meaning given to group discussion as a term to be distinguished from other types and forms of discussion, it would be to describe the participation by a *total group*, that is, all the people in a room, either following a program such as one of the many described above or in discussion generated by the group itself such as in a conference, committee, learning situation, or problem-solving objective of a public meeting. The principles brought out in Chaps. 6 and 7 would be applicable to all these situations. Some of the more important ones might be summarized here to include the following:

1. A plan for the particular meeting and its purpose should be made by the chairman and used as a guide in leading the meeting.
2. In the absence of a panel, speaker, film, or other means for laying a background for the discussion, the leader needs to give particular attention to methods of getting the discussion started and of continuing to stimulate interest as the meeting progresses. Some techniques are:
    a. The use of questions of a general or overhead nature, but sharpened toward issues and points to be brought out in the topic.
    b. Introductory remarks by the leader which will bring out points to be raised during the discussion.
    c. Prepared charts or the use at the start and during the meeting of blackboard or chart work on which main points, data, and other material pertinent to the topic will be placed.
    d. Handouts of material or points to be taken up during the discussion, passed out either before or during the meeting.
    e. Cases and examples to be discussed by the group in order to bring out principles and solutions to problems.
    f. Role-playing to dramatize cases and incidents to bring the problems and situations closer to the group for analysis and discussion.
3. The discussion should be spread throughout as many members of the group as possible.
4. The leader should exercise the minimum control necessary in order to carry out the purpose of the meeting, with the maximum

permissive atmosphere to encourage free and full contributions.
5. Speaking by all members and the leader should be done with the entire group in mind, from the standpoint of what is said, how it is said, and the attitude out of which the thought comes.

Conclusion

Having put together the principles of leadership and participation as they apply to the various types of public discussion programs and situations, it might be well to emphasize at this point that they stem from the general and basic principles of clear and analytical thinking, group analysis, interpersonal relations, and planning that were taken up in the beginning and that run throughout the pages of this book. These principles and methods vary and are modified to suit the panel, symposium, debate, lecture, forum, and group discussion generally in order best to carry out the type of program that was intended.

The good discussion leader and participant does not stop with just a mastery of the techniques and tools we have tried to supply, however important these may be. He continues to study and understand people as individuals. He is a constant student of group behavior. He keeps abreast of current topics and issues of the day in his social and business life. He develops a keen interest in being a helpful and animated contributor in all group situations. He is the Jim Weaver, average American of Chap. 1, grown to maturity in his realization of his many and complex responsibilities for participating with others in cooperative discussion in the American way of life. Having read his way through the pages of our book from the rather perplexed citizen of our first chapter, we hope that he can now meet these responsibilities with real credit to himself and the group of which he is a part.

APPLYING THIS CHAPTER

1. Will a good conference leader also be a good chairman for a panel? A forum? What additional duties and abilities are involved? Compare the two jobs fully.

2. How would you improve the handling of the forum period at the last such meeting you attended?
3. Compare the panel participant with the speaker in a symposium and in a debate.
4. From your experience as a member of a buzz group, what values did you feel came from dividing the larger group in this way? Were there any disadvantages?
5. Compare your thoughts now with those you had when you answered question 5 in Chap. 1, in which you made a list of the areas that might be improved through a study of discussion methods. To what extent do you now feel you have accomplished this improvement?

APPENDIX

Parliamentary Procedure

*Agenda for Multiple Meeting Conference
or Workshop*

*Topics and Questions for Conferences and
Discussion Programs*

Brief Cases for Discussion and Role-playing

Parliamentary Procedure

FORMAL BUSINESS MEETINGS of clubs and organizations are usually conducted according to established rules of procedure which form the basis for the systematic handling of all matters to come before the group. When such rules are followed, they provide both a fixed order for the continuity of the meeting as well as the proper consideration and disposal of each subject during the meeting. In addition, parliamentary procedure is designed to protect the minority while facilitating the will of the majority and giving each member an equal opportunity to speak.

The chairman or presiding officer needs to be conversant with the basic rules and motions which make up the body of procedure. He should at the same time be an expert discussion leader, blending together the principles of good discussion with the more formal procedural rules. Participants in a business meeting should also understand the rules and their application, in order to know what is going on and to be able to participate fully.

Order of Business

The fixed order for the continuity of a business meeting is known as the *order of business*, which should follow this sequence:

This is intended only as a brief treatment of essential principles. See Joseph F. O'Brien, *Parliamentary Law for the Layman,* Harper & Brothers, New York, 1952, and Henry M. Robert, *Rules of Order,* Scott, Foresman and Company, Chicago, 1950.

1. Opening of meeting and call to order.
2. Reading of minutes of last meeting.
3. Reading of correspondence.
4. Reports of standing committees.
5. Reports of special committees.
6. Taking up unfinished business.
7. Taking up new business.
8. Adjournment.

Parliamentary procedure is basically a system of motions which are listed in the Table of Motions in order of their rank and with essential characteristics indicated.

What to Know about Motions

Certain basic knowledge about each motion is helpful both to the chairman and member of the parliamentary group, some of which can be obtained by having a table such as the Table of Motions available at the meeting for reference.

Purpose

What will the particular motion accomplish? Or, if one has a certain objective in mind, what motion should he use? The main motion is to bring new business or a new idea to the floor. Other motions may help or facilitate its passage, hinder or postpone its passage, or bring it back for consideration again after a vote has been taken. Most of the motions fall into one of these essential purposes.

Rank or Precedence

This has to do with the order in which successive motions may be introduced after one is already on the floor. In the Table of Motions, all the motions shown above the main motion have higher rank and may be introduced after it is being considered. Each motion successively has higher rank than the ones below it in the Table of Motions. The *incidental* motions have no particular rank but are taken up whenever introduced. *Subsidiary* mo-

TABLE OF MOTIONS

Motion	Vote required	Debatable	Amend- able	Needs second	Interrupt speaker
PRIVILEGED motions:					
Fix time of next meeting	Majority	No	Yes	Yes	No
Adjourn	Majority	No	No	Yes	No
Recess	Majority	No	Yes	Yes	No
Question of privilege	Chair decides	No	No	No	Yes
Orders of the day	Chair decides	No	No	No	Yes
SUBSIDIARY motions:					
Lay on table	Majority	No	No	Yes	No
Stop debate (previous question)	⅔	No	No	Yes	No
Limit or extend debate	⅔	No	Yes	Yes	No
Postpone to definite time	Majority	Yes	Yes	Yes	No
Refer to committee	Majority	Yes	Yes	Yes	No
Amend	Majority	Yes	Yes	Yes	No
Postpone indefinitely	Majority	Yes	No	Yes	No
MAIN motion:	Majority	Yes	Yes	Yes	No
INCIDENTAL motions:					
Appeal	Majority	Yes	No	Yes	Yes
Division (for vote count)	Chair decides	No	No	No	No
Divide question	Majority	No	Yes	No	No
Withdraw motion	Majority	No	No	No	No
Point of order	Chair decides	No	No	No	Yes
Suspend rules	⅔	No	No	Yes	No
Object to consideration	⅔	No	No	No	Yes
Parliamentary inquiry	Chair decides	No	No	No	Yes
TO REOPEN AND BRING BACK BUSINESS:					
Take from table	Majority	No	No	Yes	No
Reconsider	Majority	Yes	No	Yes	Yes
Rescind or repeal	⅔	Yes	Yes	Yes	No

tions grow out of the main motion and affect its passage, with varying degrees of rank and precedence. *Privileged* motions rank still higher and thus are given this label.

Debatable

After a motion is made and accepted by the chair, it is open for discussion by the group if it is a debatable motion. Some motions may not be debated, either because of the nature of the motion or in order to better facilitate the business of the meeting.

Amendable

Once a motion is before the group in a particular form, it is acted upon as originally worded unless it is subject to amendment. The main motion or any major items of business may be amended before vote is taken; other motions must be acted upon as made and are not subject to amendment.

Vote

Most motions require a majority vote for passage. A few of the motions which have as their purpose some infringement on the freedom of discussion require a two-thirds vote for passage.

Voting is usually vocal. If this does not clearly indicate the outcome, a show of hands may be taken, or members may be asked to rise in order to be counted. Such a visible counting of the votes usually follows a call for *division* by a member of the group. If the group wishes, voting may be by closed (written) ballot.

Occasionally the chair will assume that the group wishes something done or a motion passed without a formal vote, under the principle of *general consent.* He will usually ask the group if anyone objects, and if there is no objection he assumes that the total group has consented to the decision.

In connection with voting, or with the legal right for a group to transact business at all, it must first be determined that a *quorum* is present. This is the minimum number required by the by-laws of the organization in order to have an official meeting.

Second

Most motions require a second before they can be accepted by the chair for consideration by the group. Some need not be seconded.

Interrupt Speaker

When someone has the floor and is speaking, this is generally regarded as his privilege, without interruption. In a few exceptional cases, another member may interrupt him.

The user of parliamentary procedure will realize that it is designed to help rather than hinder the smooth operation of a business meeting; that it should be interpreted and applied to meet the will of the group; and that it is the servant of the group rather than its master.

Agenda for Multiple Meeting Conference or Workshop

THE FOLLOWING is an example of an agenda or complete program for a conference or workshop extending over several days and involving a number of different subjects, speakers, and small conference breakdowns of the larger total group in attendance.

WORKSHOP IN MANAGEMENT COMMUNICATION SKILLS

The Pennsylvania State University
University Park, Pennsylvania
September 11–14, 19—

Sunday, September 11

7:00 P.M.	Registration	Nittany Lion Inn
	Buffet supper	
8:00 P.M.	Opening session	Nittany Lion Inn
	"The Place of Communication in Today's Management"	William S. Machaver

Monday, September 12

9:00 A.M.	Morning session	Conference Center
	"The Total Communication Program"	Harold P. Zelko
	Discussion	
10:00 A.M.	"Your Individual Communication Responsibilities"	Harold J. O'Brien
	Discussion	

11:00 A.M.	Organization of participants into workshop groups	
12:00 M.	Luncheon	Hetzel Union Building
	Introductory talks by all participants: "My Company's Communication Problems"	
2:00 P.M.	Afternoon session	Conference Center
	Developing speaking and listening skills	Staff
	Practice in planning, preparing, and communicating oral messages, and in listening: workshop sessions	
5:00 P.M.	Adjournment	
6:00 P.M.	Dinner	Centre Hills Country Club
	"Language and Other Communication Barriers"	Elton S. Carter

Tuesday, September 13

9:00 A.M.	Morning session	Conference Center
	Developing speaking and listening skills (continued)	Staff
12:00 M.	Luncheon	Hetzel Union Building
	"How to Write Effectively"	J. Stanley Cook
2:00 P.M.	Afternoon session	Conference Center
	Developing written communication skills	
	Workshop sessions in writing letters, reports, and other written communications	
5:00 P.M.	Adjournment	

| 6:00 P.M. | Dinner | Nittany Lion Inn |
| | "Communication Skills and Training for Better Employee Relations" | Cloyd S. Steinmetz |

Wednesday, September 14

9:00 A.M.	Morning session	Conference Session
	Developing conference skills	Staff
	Workshop sessions on principles, demonstration, and practice in leading and participating in conferences and personal relations	
12:00 M.	Luncheon	Nittany Lion Inn
	"Putting Your Communication Skills to Work"	Harold P. Zelko
2:00 P.M.	Final session	Conference Center
	Informal consideration of communication problems and application in particular companies	Staff

Topics and Questions for Conferences and Discussion Programs

Problem-solving

1. What can we do to improve company communications?
2. What's wrong with our conferences?
3. How can we improve our sales volume?
4. Can we improve our product?
5. How can we get more cooperation between departments?
6. What's wrong with morale in our company?
7. How can we reduce accident waste?
8. Should we have a new policy on promotions?
9. Should each department have athletic teams?
10. How can we better handle grievances? Reprimands?
11. How can we get more teachers?
12. Should our city have daylight saving time?
13. What can we do to promote world peace?
14. How far should Federal farm supports go?
15. Who should finance better highways?
16. What kind of armed forces should we have?
17. How can we get along best with other nations?
18. Should we have Federal price, wage, and credit controls?
19. How can we control juvenile delinquency?
20. Is the Republican or Democratic party best for the country?

Informational and Training

1. What are the uses and types of conferences?
2. What makes a good conference leader? Participant?
3. What planning is necessary for a good conference or discussion program?
4. How should visual aids be used in discussion leading?
5. What are a supervisor's duties and responsibilities?
6. How can employees best be kept informed?
7. How should a new employee be oriented to the job?
8. What are the basic principles of human relations?
9. What do you need to know about the other person for a good interview?
10. What are the basic principles of good instruction?
11. What is the present foreign policy of the United States?
12. What is the size of our armed forces?
13. What are the provisions of the Taft-Hartley law?
14. What directions is atomic research moving in?
15. What is the comparative size of the world's leading cities?
16. What are the differences between communism and democracy?
17. Who are the leaders in Russia? England?
18. What is the history of racial prejudice?
19. How long has juvenile delinquency been with us?
20. What benefits are there from training in discussion?

Brief Cases for Discussion and Role-playing

Reprimand

An employee arrived late for work, went to his machine, and started to do his job. His supervisor immediately went over to him and angrily criticized him and warned him in a loud voice in front of others. The employee had a good record for promptness and good work. He does not reply.

Grievance

While the supervisor was seated at his desk, an employee approached him very much upset about a problem in the work scene. Obviously busy, the supervisor waited to greet the man until he had seemed to state his problem. Finally the supervisor looked up and said, "Why are you always complaining about little things?" The supervisor had not heard the man and did not know the facts. "Let's talk about it another time," he said.

Problem Employee

One worker takes frequent rest periods and returns late from lunch habitually. His production record is higher than the average of the work group. What should the supervisor do?

Communism

A member of a union was identified as a member of the Communist party, and the company dismissed him from employment. He was otherwise a good worker. The union's executive committee meets to decide whether to appeal the case to have the employee reinstated.

Instructions

After a supervisor spent what he thought to be a sufficient amount of time explaining a work operation, one of the workers said that he didn't understand what to do. The supervisor replied that he should keep his ears open and refused to explain further. Whose fault is it?

Student

(a) A student in a fraternity has been violating the social rules of the fraternity and the university. The fraternity president calls him in for interview. The Dean of Men also calls him in.

(b) Another student has an excellent record but refuses to dress properly at dinner and other functions.

(c) The student advisory committee on scholarship at X University meets to consider the question of awarding scholarships to deserving athletes who are not necessarily good students.

Leadership

A supervisor is known to play poker with his workers and to advise them concerning matters of personal and domestic nature. Should he do this?

Cooperation

Supervisor A notices that Supervisor B is using more and more of his share of the storage space that they were to share equally. What should Supervisor A do about it?

Customer Relations

A power company service man who stops work at 5:00 P.M. makes an emergency call at a customer's home to repair a range, arriving at 4:45 P.M. Obviously upset, he proceeds to act in a discourteous manner with the customer and tries to get her to postpone the repair until the next day. The customer needs the range to cook supper that night.

Selected Bibliography

Books

Baird, A. C., *Argumentation, Discussion, and Debate,* McGraw-Hill Book Company, Inc., New York, 1950.

Bales, R. F., *Interaction Process Analysis,* Addison-Wesley Publishing Company, Cambridge, Mass., 1950.

Beardsley, M. C., *Thinking Straight,* revised, Prentice-Hall, Inc., Englewood Cliffs, N.J., 1956.

Beckman, R. O., *How to Train Supervisors,* Harper & Brothers, New York, 1942.

Braden, W. W., and E. Brandenburg, *Oral Decision-making,* Harper & Brothers, New York, 1955.

Cantor, N., *Learning through Discussion,* Human Relations for Industry, Buffalo, N.Y., 1951.

Cartwright, D., and A. Zander, eds., *Group Dynamics: Research and Theory,* Row, Peterson & Company, Evanston, Ill., 1953.

Clapp, J. M., *Effective Talking in Conference,* The Ronald Press Company, New York, 1948.

Cooper, A. M., *How to Conduct Conferences,* McGraw-Hill Book Company, Inc., New York, 1946.

Dewey, J., *How We Think,* revised, D. C. Heath and Company, Boston, 1933.

Dooher, M. J., and V. Marquis, eds., *Effective Communication on the Job,* American Management Association, New York, 1956.

Ewbank, H. L., and J. J. Auer, *Discussion and Debate,* revised, Appleton-Century-Crofts, Inc., New York, 1951.

Fansler, T., *Creative Power through Discussion,* Harper & Brothers, New York, 1950.

Given, W. B., Jr., *Bottom-up Management,* Harper & Brothers, New York, 1949.

Gordon, T., *Group-centered Leadership,* Houghton Mifflin Company, Boston, 1955.

Guetzkow, H., ed., *Groups, Leadership, and Men,* Carnegie Institute of Technology Press, Pittsburgh, 1951.

Haiman, F. S., *Group Leadership and Democratic Action,* Houghton Mifflin Company, Boston, 1951.

Hannaford, E. S., *Conference Leadership in Business and Industry,* McGraw-Hill Book Company, Inc., New York, 1945.

Hare, P., E. F. Borgatta, and R. F. Bales, *Small Groups: Studies in Social Interaction,* Alfred A. Knopf, Inc., New York, 1955.

Howell, W. S., and D. K. Smith, *Discussion,* The Macmillan Company, New York, 1956.

Lee, I., *How to Talk with People,* Harper & Brothers, New York, 1952.

Lee, I., *Customs and Crises in Communication,* Harper & Brothers, New York, 1954.

Maier, N. R. F., *Principles of Human Relations,* John Wiley & Sons, Inc., New York, 1952.

McBurney, J. H., and K. G. Hance, *Discussion in Human Affairs,* Harper & Brothers, New York, 1950.

Morrison, S. N., *et al., Conference Leader's Source Book,* National Foremen's Institute, New London, Conn., 1946.

O'Brien, J. F., *Parliamentary Law for the Layman,* Harper & Brothers, New York, 1952.

Oliver, R. T., *Psychology of Persuasive Speech,* revised, Longmans, Green & Co., Inc., New York, 1957.

Oliver, R. T., D. Dickey, and H. P. Zelko, *Communicative Speech,* revised, The Dryden Press, Inc., New York, 1955.

Osborn, A. F., *Applied Imagination,* Charles Scribner's Sons, New York, 1953.

Peters, R. W., *Communication within Industry,* Harper & Brothers, New York, 1950.

Phillips, D., *Oral Communication in Business,* McGraw-Hill Book Company, Inc., New York, 1954.

Pigors, P., *Effective Communication in Industry,* National Association of Manufacturers, New York, 1949.

Pigors, P. and F., *The Incident Process: Case Studies in Management Development,* Bureau of National Affairs, Washington, D.C., 1955.

Planty, E. G., W. S. McCord, and C. A. Efferson, *Training Employees and Managers,* The Ronald Press Company, New York, 1948.

Redfield, C., *Communication in Management,* University of Chicago Press, Chicago, 1953.

Robert, H., *Rules of Order,* revised, Scott, Foresman and Company, Chicago, 1950.

Sattler, W. M., and N. E. Miller, *Discussion and Conference,* Prentice-Hall, Inc., New York, 1954.

Stigers, M. F., *Making Conference Programs Work,* McGraw-Hill Book Company, Inc., New York, 1949.

Strauss, B. and F., *New Ways to Better Meetings,* The Viking Press, Inc., New York, 1951.

Sturgis, Alice F., *Sturgis Standard Code of Parliamentary Procedure,* McGraw-Hill Book Company, Inc., New York, 1950.

Utterback, W. E., *Group Thinking and Conference Leadership,* Rinehart & Company, Inc., New York, 1950.

Wagner, R. H., and C. C. Arnold, *Handbook of Group Discussion,* Houghton Mifflin Company, Boston, 1950.

Walser, F., *Art of Conference,* revised, Harper & Brothers, New York, 1948.

Whyte, W. H., *Is Anybody Listening?* Simon and Schuster, Inc., New York, 1952.

Wolff, J., *The Production Conference,* Harper & Brothers, New York, 1944.

Zelko, H. P., and H. J. O'Brien, *Management-Employee Communication in Action,* Howard Allen, Inc., Cleveland, 1957.

Pamphlets and Industrial Materials

Argyris, C., *Role Playing in Action,* New York State School of Industrial and Labor Relations, Ithaca, N.Y., 1951.

Bradford, L. P., and S. M. Corey, *Leadership and Participation in Large Group Meetings,* Bulletin 4, National Education Association, Washington, D.C., 1951.

Educator's Washington Dispatch, *Two Lessons in Group Dynamics,* Arthur C. Croft Publications, New London, Conn., 1951.

Lippitt, G. L., and W. H. Schmidt, *My Group and I*, Arthur C. Croft Publications, New London, Conn., 1952.

Zelko, H. P., *How to Hold Meetings and Conferences* and *Are You a Good Listener?*, National Foremen's Institute, New London, Conn., 1951.

E. I. Du Pont de Nemours & Co., Inc., *Discussion Leading*, Wilmington, Del., 1952.

Esso Standard Oil Co., *Conference Leader Training*, Esso Training Center, Elizabeth, N.J., 1947.

Johnson & Johnson, *Conference Leadership Training*, New Brunswick, N.J., 1954.

U.S. Department of the Air Force, *Conference Leadership*, AF Manual 50-8, Washington, D.C., 1951.

Periodicals and Special Studies

American Management Association, *Improving Management Communication*, New York, 1950.

Bales, R. F., "In Conference," *Harvard Business Review*, vol. 32, March–April 1954.

Bales, R. F., "How People Interact in Conferences," *Scientific American*, vol. 192, March, 1955.

Barnlund, D. C., "Experiments in Leadership Training for Decision-making Discussion Groups," Ph.D. dissertation, Northwestern University, Evanston, Ill., 1951.

Berkowitz, L., "Sharing Leadership in Small Decision-making Groups," *Journal of Abnormal and Social Psychology*, vol. 48, 1953.

Dickens, M., and M. Heffernan, "Experimental Research in Group Discussion," *Quarterly Journal of Speech*, vol. 35, February, 1949.

Giffin, K., "Current Directions in Discussion Research," *The Gavel*, vol. 36, January, 1954.

Goode, C. E., "Significant Research on Leadership," *Personnel*, vol. 28, March, 1951.

Gunderson, R. G., "Group Dynamics—Hope or Hoax," *Quarterly Journal of Speech*, vol. 36, February, 1950.

Haiman, F. S., "Concepts of Leadership," *Quarterly Journal of Speech*, vol. 39, October, 1953.

Heyns, R. W., "Effects of Variation in Leadership on Participation Behavior in Group Discussion," Conference Research Project, Ann Arbor, Mich., 1948 (mimeographed release).

Kelman, H. C., "Group Dynamics—Neither Hope Nor Hoax," *Quarterly Journal of Speech*, vol. 36, October, 1950.

Keltner, J., "Committee Dynamics," *The Gavel*, vol. 32, November, 1949; March and January, 1950.

Kriesberg, M., "Executives Evaluate Administrative Conferences," *Advanced Management*, vol. 15, March, 1950.

Lee, I. J., "Procedure for Coercing Agreement," *Harvard Business Review*, vol. 32, January–February, 1954.

Lippitt, R., and R. K. White, "An Experimental Study of Leadership and Group Life," in T. M. Newcomb and E. L. Hartley, eds., *Readings in Social Psychology*, Henry Holt and Company, Inc., New York, 1947.

Machaver, W. V., and F. E. Fischer, "The Leader's Role in Role Playing," *Journal of Industrial Training*, vol. 7, January–February, 1953.

Maier, N. R. F., "The Quality of Group Decisions as Influenced by the Discussion Leader," *Human Relations*, vol. 3, 1950.

Mathews, A., "Ten Minute Training Tips," Hamilton Watch Company, Lancaster, Pa., 1954.

Miller, N. E., "The Effect of Group Size on Decision-making Discussions," Ph.D. dissertation, University of Michigan, Ann Arbor, Mich., 1951.

Moody, K. A., "Role Playing as a Training Technique," *Journal of Industrial Training*, vol. 7, January–February, 1953.

National Association of Manufacturers, *Casebook of Employee Communications in Action* and *Employee Communications*, New York, 1950.

National Industrial Conference Board, Studies in Personnel Policy, *Techniques of Conference Leadership*, No. 77, New York, 1946; *Communication within the Management Group*, No. 80, New York, 1947; *Communicating with Employees*, No. 129, New York, 1952.

O'Brien, J. F., "A Definition and Classification of the Forms of Discussion," *Quarterly Journal of Speech*, vol. 25, April, 1939.

O'Brien, J. F., "Don't Shove, Mr. Knowles: Parliamentary Law is Basically Sound," *Today's Speech*, vol. 2, January, 1954.

Peterman, J. N., "Verbal Participation—Its Relation to Decision Satisfaction and the Leader Function in Decision-making Groups," Conference Research Project, Ann Arbor, Mich., 1948 (mimeographed release).

Phillips, J. D., "Report on Discussion 66," *Adult Education Journal,* vol. 7, October, 1948.

Planty, E. G., and W. Machaver, "Upward Communication: A Project in Executive Development," *Personnel,* vol. 28, January, 1952.

Utterback, W. E., "The Moderator's Function in Group Thinking," *Quarterly Journal of Speech,* vol. 34, December, 1948.

Watson, G., "Do Groups Think More Efficiently than Individuals?" *Journal of Abnormal and Social Psychology,* vol. 23, October–December, 1928.

Wilson, C., "An Experimental Study of Correlates of Emergent Leadership in Leaderless Problem-solving Discussion," Ph.D. Dissertation, The Pennsylvania State University, University Park, Pa., 1952.

Zelko, H. P., "Training Conference Leaders for Industry and Government," *Southern Speech Journal,* vol. 14, March, 1949.

Zelko, H. P., "Conference Management: Beware of the Gimmicks," *Advanced Management,* vol. 19, December, 1954.

Zelko, H. P., "How Effective Are Your Company Communications?," *Advanced Management,* vol. 21, February, 1956.

Visual Aids

THE VISUAL MATERIALS described below and on the following pages can be used to illustrate and supplement material in this book. Both motion pictures and filmstrips are included in the visual bibliography, the character of each being indicated by the abbreviations MP and FS. Immediately following such identification is the name of the producer; if different, the name of the distributor is also given. Abbreviations used for these names are identified in the list of sources at the end of the bibliography. In many instances, the films can be borrowed or rented from local or state 16mm film libraries. A nation-wide list of these sources is given in *A Directory of 3,300 16mm Film Libraries*, available for 70 cents from the Superintendent of Documents, U.S. Government Printing Office, Washington 25, D.C. Unless otherwise indicated, the motion pictures are 16mm sound black-and-white films and the filmstrips are 35mm, black-and-white, and silent. The length of motion pictures is given in minutes (min) and of filmstrips in frames (fr).

Readers should also consult *Educational Film Guide* and *Filmstrip Guide*, standard reference catalogs available in most school, college, and public libraries.

All I Need Is a Conference (MP, GE/Strauss, 1954, 30 min). Dramatizes a situation of department heads being called together to solve a pressing company problem—some indifferent, some hostile, some harassed and worried, some too shy to speak. Recognizing these personality differences, the skilled conference leader helps all conferees to participate in thinking the problem through and agreeing upon a solution.

Belonging to the Group (MP, EBF, 1952, 16 min, color or b&w). Explains the meaning of the idea of respect and its essential relation to living in a democracy, the origin and development of some barriers to respect, and ways of eliminating such barriers.

Bridges for Ideas (MP, USC, 1951, 28 min). Describes communications media as bridges for ideas and explains the importance of understanding the functions and techniques of language, motion pictures, radio and television, fine arts, and other means of communicating information and concepts.

Buzz Session (MP, UAW, 1953, 22 min). Illustrates the "buzz session" or small discussion group method as it is used in the summer schools of the United Automobile Workers union.

Communications Primer (MP, MMA, 1954, 22 min, color). Illustrates recent theories on communications, and explains the nature of communication and its operations in modern civilization.

Discussion in Democracy (MP, Coronet, 1949, 10 min, color or b&w). Illustrates through a group discussion by students the basic elements of any discussion—preparation, planning, and personalities.

Discussion of the Social Sciences (MP, EBF, 1950, 22 min). A film record of an unrehearsed discussion in a first-year college class in social science. Points up the role of the instructor as leader and the contributions of the students to a well-planned, skilfully executed discussion.

Discussion Technique (MP, US Defense/UWF, 1950, 28 min). Shows how to conduct a discussion by forum, symposium, debate, panel, conference, and committee techniques and how to stimulate independent thinking and free interchange of ideas among enlisted personnel.

Does It Matter What You Think? (MP, BIS, 1945, 15 min). Discusses and illustrates the factors which help form public opinion, including the media of mass communication and the exchange of opinions among individuals.

Experiment (MP, GM, 1947, 12 min). Humorous explanation of how to influence people by gentle persuasion. Live-action photography and cartoon animation.

Experimental Studies in Social Climates of Groups (MP, Iowa U, 1953, 31 min). Shows behavior of groups of boys organized in clubs run on democratic principles, as an autocracy, and as a laissez-faire group. Shows responses when groups are changed from one type to another.

How Not to Conduct a Meeting (MP, GM, 1941, 10 min). Burlesque of common errors and omissions frequently encountered in poorly planned luncheon meetings.

How to Conduct a Discussion (MP, EBF, 1953, 23 min). Explains and illustrates eleven principles to be observed by discussion leaders in order to achieve effective and satisfying group discussion.

How to Conduct a Meeting (MP, USIA/UWF, 1950, 20 min). Shows the proper procedures of parliamentary law to be followed in conducting a meeting so that the decisions will be representative of the majority.

How to Lead a Discussion (FS, Sch C, 1948, 81 fr with script). Pictures of the process and techniques of group discussion.

How to Think (MP, Coronet, 1951, 10 min, color or b&w). Explains through a dramatized incident the elements of concentration, observation, memory, and logical reasoning.

How We Learn (MP, Coronet, 1951, 10 min, color or b&w). Analyzes the process of learning as being based upon two components: "readiness" and "materials." Primarily for high-school students.

Making Yourself Understood (MP, EBF, 1954, 14 min). Uses a case study to analyze and illustrate the basic factors of communication, including predispositions of people as well as the content and style of the message.

Meeting in Session (MP, TC, 1953, 20 min). Consists of two sequences: (1) five nurses discussing staffing problems with an autocratic supervisor and (2) the same group working democratically to solve its problems.

Organizing Discussion Groups (MP, EBF, 1953, 21 min). Explains the importance of discussion groups in modern society, outlines the steps to follow in organizing a group, and explains some of the problems and possible solutions.

Our Invisible Committees (MP, Nat Tr Lab, 1951, 25 min). Explores the point of view that one of the important obstacles to group thought and decision-making is the conflict of social pressures which operate within individuals during a meeting. Presents a case study of such a group.

Parliamentary Procedure (MP, Coronet, 1952, 11 min, color or b&w). Shows parliamentary procedures used in a civic meeting, including reading of minutes, reports of standing committees, unfinished business, new business, etc. Illustrates the handling of motions and amendments to motions.

Parliamentary Rules of Order (MP, Mich U, 1954, 59 fr). Explains the necessity for rules of order and the use of parliamentary procedure. Gives illustrations of common procedural questions that arise in meetings and the answers to these questions.

Personnel Management (MP series, McGraw, 1953). The following four films in this series (each with a follow-up filmstrip) illustrate principles and procedures of conferences and discussions. Titles are:

Communications (12 min)
Employment Interview (11 min)
Grievance Hearing (15 min)
Supervisory Conferences (14 min)

Role-playing in Human Relations Training (MP, Nat Tr Lab, 1949, 27 min). Spontaneous enactment of three human relations situations illustrating techniques essential to role-playing.

Room for Discussion (MP, EBF, 1952, 25 min). Examines the nature and function of discussion in its personal and social aspects. Describes the process of discussion and gives illustrations of discussion techniques.

Rumor Clinic (FS, ADL, 1948, 34 fr with script). Demonstrates the ways in which rumors are compounded. Requires audience participation.

Social Process (MP, EBF, 1952, 20 min). Professor Harold D. Lasswell conducting a seminar on the patterns of behavior common to all cultures and explaining the concept that "man seeks values through institutions using resources."

Take the Fourth Part (MP, Baptist, 1955, 10 min). Shows how to prepare and present a discussion for a Training Union of the Southern Baptist Convention.

Unconscious Motivation (MP, Assn, 1949, 38 min). Demonstrates how unconscious motives can influence and direct everyday thoughts, feelings, and actions and explains how psychological techniques can be used to detect the presence of troublesome, repressed ideas.

What Do You Think? (MP series, CNFB/McGraw, 1953). Seven films, six minutes each, dramatizing problem situations, leaving discussion and resolution to the audience. Titles are:

Getting What You're After
Having Your Say
Honest Truth
Majority Vote
One Man's Opinion

Public's Business
Who's Running Things?

Working for Better Public Health through Recognition of Feelings (MP, USPHS, 1953, 25 min). Shows good and poor human relations situations in public health work, discusses the problems involved, and emphasizes the importance of recognizing feelings of people.

Main Sources of Films

ADL—Anti-Defamation League of B'nai Brith, 515 Madison Ave., New York 22

Assn—Association Films, Inc., 347 Madison Ave., New York 17

Baptist—Baptist Book Stores, 127 Ninth Ave., Nashville 3, Tenn.

BIS—British Information Services, 30 Rockefeller Plaza, New York 20

CNFB—National Film Board of Canada, 630 Fifth Ave., New York 20

Coronet—Coronet Instructional Films, Coronet Bldg., Chicago 1

EBF—Encyclopaedia Britannica Films, Inc., 1150 Wilmette Ave., Wilmette, Ill.

GE—General Electric Co., 1 River Rd., Schenectady 5, N.Y.

GM—General Motors Corp., 3044 W. Grand Blvd., Detroit 2, and 405 Montgomery St., San Francisco 4

Iowa U—State University of Iowa, Iowa City, Iowa

McGraw—McGraw-Hill Book Company, Inc., Text-Film Dept., 330 W. 42nd St., New York 36

Mich U—University of Michigan, Ann Arbor, Mich.

MMA—Museum of Modern Art, 11 W. 53rd St., New York 19

Nat Tr Lab—National Training Laboratory in Group Development, 1201 16th St., N.W., Washington, D.C.

Sch C—Schauffler College of Religious and Social Work, 5115 Fowler Ave., Cleveland, Ohio

Strauss—Henry Strauss & Co., 668 Fifth Ave., New York 19

TC—Teachers College, Columbia University, 525 W. 120th St., New York 27

UAW—United Automobile Workers, 8000 E. Jefferson Ave., Detroit 14

USC—University of Southern California, Los Angeles

US Defense—U.S. Department of Defense, Washington 25, D.C.

USIA—U.S. Information Agency, Washington 25, D.C. (Films distributed in the United States by United World Films, Inc.)

USPHS—U.S. Public Health Service, Washington 25, D.C.

UWF—United World Films, Inc., 1445 Park Ave., New York 29

Index